The Mediterranean
Diet Recipe Book

Affordable, Healthy and Super-Amazing Dishes
for Everyday Enjoyment I including Breakfast,
Lunch, Dinner & Desserts I 14-Day Meal Plan

Tony R. Harrington

ISBN - 9798366510943

Table of Contents

EXCLUSIVE BONUS

40 Weight Loss Recipes

&

14 Days Meal Plan

Scan the QR-Code and receive
the FREE download:

Introduction

We know that overall health and wellbeing is the aim in life. That means exercising regularly, maintaining a low stress level, kicking out unhealthy habits, such as smoking and drug taking, and of course it also means eating a healthy and varied diet every single day.

Does that mean you can never give yourself a treat? Of course not. But, it does mean that 9 times out of 10, you should focus upon clean, healthy foods and cooking yourself. Takeouts are a treat occasionally, for sure, but if you eat them too often, you're going to find yourself in a pretty unhealthy state. If you cook for yourself most of the time, you'll actually start to enjoy it, you'll save money, and you'll notice how much healthier you feel.

So, while focusing upon health and wellbeing is a very positive step, you have to make sure that you're focusing upon the right things. Hands up who has ever tried a fad diet. Most hands are probably up right now.

The truth is that nobody tries a fad diet and sticks to it over the long-haul. There is a reason they're called 'fad' diets – because they're completely unsustainable. They make you miserable, and we all know that life is far too short to be miserable!

Instead, you need to look towards a diet that is easy to follow. You should also avoid calling it a 'diet'. You simply need a healthier lifestyle.

While the term 'Mediterranean Diet' has the word 'diet' in it, it's far from that; it's a lifestyle change that will help you to work towards optimum health and wellbeing, while giving you a true appreciation for good, healthy, seasonal, and clean foods.

Welcome to The Mediterranean Diet

This book is about the Mediterranean Diet. As the name suggests, this is a healthy eating regime that is inspired by the diets of the Mediterranean region.

Cuisine from this region of the world is focused towards seasonal produce, home cooking, and the healthier side of life in general. This means that the amount of unhealthy food you eat is limited (never cut out completely, because we all deserve an occasional treat), and the healthy stuff makes up the bulk of your regular intake instead. Produce is eaten as fresh as possible, organic as far as you can, and seasonal. That means it's as tasty as it can possibly be, while retaining all the vitamins and minerals.

When you follow this healthy eating routine, increase your exercise levels every week, and kick out unhealthy habits, you'll notice how much better you feel and you'll do a lot to drastically reduce your risk factors for serious disease.

So, we know that the Mediterranean Diet is inspired by foods grown and enjoyed in this region of the world, but which particular countries and when did it start?

The diet began around the 1960s but it has grown in popularity drastically over the last few years, as we've become far more aware of healthy foods and what we need to do to ensure that we stay on the right side of the health and fitness argument. The diet is inspired by foods that are regularly grown and served in Greece, France, Spain, and Italy. If you've ever visited one of these countries, you'll know that their local cuisine is delicious. That's what you can expect by following this diet!

The good news is that there is no weighing, counting, or strict coloured days when you follow the Mediterranean Diet. It's basically a set of guidelines that encourage you to make healthy choices and to choose fresh produce to create your own home cooked meals. That means it's completely different to fad diets that we know simply don't work. It's much easier to follow, far more sustainable, and it has a huge amount of scope in terms of the delicious meals you can make at home, in the comfort of your own kitchen.

If you're not the greatest cook, don't worry! Throughout this book we're going to share plenty of truly delicious recipes that you can make from scratch, using fresh produce easily found in your local supermarket's fresh fruit and vegetable section.

You'll notice that most meals are made up of fresh vegetables, fresh fruits, fresh fish, unsaturated fats, cereals, beans, nuts, legumes, and grains. Again, you don't have to weigh anything and you simply make good and strong decisions around your food intake. You'll also notice that you can eat rice, bread, and pasta on the Mediterranean Diet too - fill up and you won't be hungry!

Foods to Eat on The Mediterranean Diet

The first thing most people do when deciding whether or not a diet is for them is to look at the foods you can eat versus the food you shouldn't eat. When you look at the list of foods you can eat below, you'll see just how much easier it is to follow the Mediterranean Diet and how you can still enjoy a lot of your favourite foods.

Remember, you can treat yourself with a takeaway occasionally, but make sure that it's not a regular thing. Once a month, go for it. Moderation is key here. The Mediterranean Diet is a long-term lifestyle change that needs to be sensible and sustainable for you to follow. Telling you to never eat a pizza or a bar of chocolate again is just unrealistic. We're not telling you that, because we know that you want to enjoy the food you eat. But, you have to remember that if you want to lose weight and remain healthy over the long-term, you need to cut out the unhealthy stuff for the overwhelming majority of the time and only enjoy treats occasionally and in moderation.

It will get easier the more you do it.

When following the Mediterranean Diet, you can eat:
- Fresh fruits
- Fresh vegetables
- Seeds, such as sunflower seeds
- Nuts, e.g. hazelnuts, almonds, macadamia nuts and walnuts
- Olives and olive oil
- Avocados
- Avocado oil
- Legumes, such as lentils and peas
- Potatoes

- Brown or wholegrain bread
- Wholegrains, including wholegrain pasta
- Herbs and spices
- Seafood, including fresh fish such as tuna, trout, crab, and salmon
- Unsweetened tea and coffee
- Red wine - no more than 1 glass per day

In moderation you can eat:
- Cheese
- Eggs
- Red meat
- Poultry
- Yogurt

When selecting your foods, make sure that you go for the freshest options possible. Organic is always a good route here, because you know that they're going to maintain all their vitamins and minerals and there is nothing added in, to lengthen life, etc.

Also, remember to drink plenty of water throughout the day.

While most of the foods listed above are those regularly used and found in Mediterranean countries, you can easily find them worldwide in supermarkets and grocery stores. It's a good idea to shop at farmer's markets and regular fruit and vegetable markets if you can, as this is where you'll find the tastiest options for your homemade dishes. The flavour will shine through!

While you don't have to aim for 5 a day, or whatever the number is these days, you should make sure that you get as many fresh fruit and vegetables as you can every day.

Foods You Should Avoid on The Mediterranean Diet

Remember, you can have treats occasionally but these are the foods that you should do your best to avoid while following the Mediterranean Diet.

- Trans fats
- Refined grains, and yes, that does mean white bread unfortunately!
- Refined oils
- Foods which are labelled 'low fat' or anything which says you can eat it while on a diet
- Sweetened beverages, such as lemonade or cola
- Processed meats, such as burgers
- Foods which contain unnatural sugar, such as chocolate, sweets, etc.

These foods might be a little upsetting considering that most people enjoy a cookie or some ice cream occasionally but remember that you should avoid them as much as you possibly can, most of the time. Again, treats are fine but you shouldn't make a habit of it.

How to Start on The Mediterranean Diet

Before you start the diet, it's a good idea to do a little preparation. By doing that, you'll be able to get your new healthy lifestyle off to the best possible start.

Clear out your kitchen cupboards, refrigerator and freezer of any of the 'do not eat' items above and make sure it's stocked with the items that you can eat freely or in moderation. That way, you'll be far less tempted to eat things which you know are going to cause problems to your efforts.

You should also:
- **Meal planning** - This doesn't mean you need to get a clipboard and write every meal and snack down, but it does give you a little guidance and means that you're less likely to "fall off the wagon" if you're late home from work and have no idea what to cook for dinner. It also saves money because you know what you need to buy to create the meal.
- **Bulk buy ingredients** - It's a good idea to go shopping once per week and actually go to the supermarket or market, rather than ordering online. That way, you can see what you're buying. You'll also save money because you're not buying odd things every other day. Once you start meal planning, you'll also be able to create a list of what to buy and go from there.
- **Organic produce is the way forward** - We've mentioned a few times that you should go for organic items as much as you can, and that's a very strong piece of advice to follow on the Mediterranean Diet. Look for deals and stock up for your week's meals. This type of produce is packed with vitamins

and minerals and doesn't have the extras that some things have, which make them last longer.

- **Become food label savvy** - By learning how to read food labels you won't accidentally eat something that's going to cause a problem to your new healthy lifestyle. It might take a while to understand food labels completely but with practice you'll get there. It's a very good habit to get into and will help you to understand what is in your foods.

- **Don't worry if you're not the best chef** - The recipes we're going to show you shortly will give you confidence to start cooking for yourself. You don't have to be the best chef in the world to make these recipes, they're pretty easy! You'll also find that the more you cook for yourself, the better at it you'll become.

- **Learn to understand when you're full** - Eat slowly and learn to recognise when your stomach is full. That way, you won't overeat and you'll enjoy your meals so much more. There's no fun in feeling too full and there's certainly no fun in the gastric disturbances afterwards! By learning to know when you're full, you have total control over your food.

- **Be sure to drink plenty of water** - Water is vital for overall health and wellbeing and it's very easy to forget that you've not had a drink for several hours! When you're busy, make sure that you keep a refillable bottle of water with you and keep sipping. Not only will this aid with weight loss but it will help you to achieve optimum health and well-being regardless. You will also probably notice that you have a lot more energy.

Look Forward to a Healthier Life

Now you know what the Mediterranean Diet is and you've seen the types of foods you can at versus the ones you should avoid, you should have a pretty clear picture of what it entails.

How do you feel about it now? Hopefully you're excited and ready to get started!

Throughout the rest of this book you'll find countless delicious recipes for you to enjoy. You can create all of these recipes very easily with ingredients you'll find locally, and remember mix and match your meals over the course of the week. Variation is key if you want to enjoy the food you consume every single day. You'll certainly find your favourites, but remember to mix things up occasionally and look for new favourites too!

So, without further ado, let's get ready to start your journey into the Mediterranean Diet.

EXCLUSIVE BONUS

40 Weight Loss Recipes

&

14 Days Meal Plan

Scan the QR-Code and receive
the FREE download:

Mediterranean Diet Breakfast Recipes

Breakfast is the most important meal of the day – surely you've heard that old adage! Below you will find some delicious recipes you can make quickly and easily for breakfast, working hand in hand with the Mediterranean Diet's general guidelines.

Remember to mix up your morning meal across the week and you'll never get bored!

Banana & Tahini Shakes

Serves 3
Calories – 150, carbs – 2.8g, protein – 6g, fat – 7g

Ingredients

♦ 350ml / 1.5 cups of almond milk (unsweetened)
♦ 2 frozen bananas, sliced
♦ 100ml / 0.25 cups tahini
♦ A handful of ice cubes
♦ 0.5 tsp ground cinnamon

Method

1. Place all the ingredients in a blender (except for the cinnamon) and combine until smooth
2. Pour into serving glasses and sprinkle with cinnamon

Morning Vegetables & Eggs

Serves 1
Calories – 222, carbs – 11g, protein – 11g, fat – 13g

Ingredients

- 1 tbsp olive oil
- 1 yellow pepper, sliced
- 2 spring onions/scallions, sliced
- 8 cherry tomatoes, cut into quarters
- 2 tbsp sliced black peppers
- 1 tbsp capers
- 0.25 tsp dried oregano
- 4 eggs
- Salt and pepper

Method

1. Take a large frying pan heat the oil over a medium temperature
2. Add the peppers and scallions/spring onions and cook until softened
3. Add the capers, tomatoes, and olives, cooking for another minute
4. Crack the eggs into the pan and scramble with a fork
5. Add the seasoning to your preferences
6. Stir the eggs until they're cooked to your liking

Fruity Potato Hash

Serves 2
Calories – 216, carbs – 12, protein – 14g, fat – 14g

Ingredients

- 1 tbsp avocado oil, plus another 2 tsp divided
- 400g/14oz quartered Brussels sprouts
- 1 cubed sweet potato
- 2 garlic cloves, minced
- 1 onion, chopped
- 4 medium eggs
- 1 tbsp dried sage
- 400g/14oz apple, chopped
- 250g/9oz spinach
- Salt and pepper

Method

1. Preheat your oven to 200C / 428F
2. Line a baking sheet with parchment and add the potatoes and Brussels sprouts, with a tbsp of the oil drizzled over the top
3. Season to your liking and place in the oven for 25 minutes
4. Add the rest of the oil to a large skillet pan and use a medium temperature to heat
5. Once hot, add the garlic, sage, and apple and cook for 4 minutes
6. Transfer the sprouts and potato from the baking sheet into the skillet and stir well
7. Set aside
8. Add a small amount of oil to another skillet pan and crack the eggs inside
9. Cook the eggs to your preference
10. Serve the eggs on the top of the hash

Majoon Smoothies

Serves 4
Calories – 110, carbs – 2, protein – 3g, fat – 3g

Ingredients

- 5 dates, pitted
- 1 banana
- A handful of pistachio nuts
- A large handful of walnuts
- 0.25 tsp ground cinnamon
- 0.5 tsp vanilla extract
- 300ml/1.5 cups of almond milk
- A large handful of ice cubes

Method

1. Take a large blender and add all ingredient inside
2. Blend for around 1 minute on a high setting, until a smooth consistency is formed
3. Divide between 4 glasses and enjoy

Spinach & Artichoke Pancake

Serves 4
Calories – 213, carbs – 20g, protein – 9.3g, fat – 14g

Ingredients

- 2 tbsp olive oil
- 8 eggs
- 1 tbsp mustard, Dijon works best
- 2 garlic cloves, minced
- 5 chopped artichokes
- 125g/4.5oz sour cream
- 500g/17oz spinach
- 250g/8.5oz grated cheese

Method

1. Preheat the oven to 200C / 428F
2. Combine the eggs, half the cheese, mustard, sour cream and the seasoning in a large bowl and combine
3. Set aside
4. Take a large frying pan and add the olive oil over a medium heat
5. Cook the artichokes until a little brown
6. Add the spinach and the garlic to the pan and stir well, cooking for 2 minutes
7. Pour the egg mixture over the pan and ensure it's evenly distributed
8. Add the cheese over the top of the pan
9. Cook for a few minutes, until the eggs are cooked as you like them
10. Place the pan into the oven and cook for around 15 minutes
11. Allow to cool and then slice

Cheese & Spinach Breakfast Casserole

Serves 4
Calories – 186, carbs – 3.5g, protein – 8g, fat – 10g

Ingredients

- 4 tsp olive oil
- 10 medium eggs
- 450ml/1.8 cups milk
- 400g/14oz fresh spinach
- 2 garlic cloves, minced
- 4 chopped artichoke hearts
- 250g/8oz feta cheese, crumbled
- 1 tsp fresh lemon juice
- 1 tbsp dill, chopped
- 1 tsp lemon juice
- 1 tsp dried oregano
- Salt and pepper

Method

1. Preheat the oven to 190C / 374F
2. Add 1tbsp olive oil to a large skillet pan over a medium heat
3. Add the spinach and garlic and cook for 3 minutes
4. Take a baking dish and transfer the mixture to the bottom, along with the artichokes
5. In a mixing bowl, combine the lemon juice, milk, herbs, eggs, and seasoning
6. Pour over the top of the dish and make sure everything is even
7. Add the cheese over the top and cook in the oven for 30 minutes

Shakshuka

Serves 4
Calories – 400, carbs – 17g, protein – 11g, fat – 13.5g

Ingredients

- 2 tbsp olive oil
- 5 medium eggs
- 1 onion, chopped
- 1 can peeled tomatoes
- 3 garlic cloves, minced
- 1 tbsp harissa paste
- 2 tbsp tomato paste
- 1 tsp cumin
- 0.5 tsp salt

Method

1. Take a large skillet pan and add the olive oil over a medium heat
2. Once hot, add the onion and cook for 2 minutes
3. Add the harissa paste, cumin, tomato paste, garlic and salt and stir well, cooking for another minute
4. Add the tomatoes and simmer for 10 minutes
5. Set the pan aside and create five holes in the cooked mixture
6. Take one egg and crack into one of the holes, repeating for the rest
7. Stir a little of the tomato mixture over the egg whites
8. Add the pan back to the heat and cook for 15 minutes

Quinoa For The Mornings

Serves 4
Calories – 307, carbs – 33g, protein – 9.5g, fat – 7g

Ingredients

- 250ml/1 cup milk
- 2 tbsp honey
- 150g/5oz chopped raw almonds
- 150g/5oz quinoa
- 1 tsp vanilla extract
- 1 tsp cinnamon
- 5 chopped apricots
- 2 chopped dates

Method

1. Add the almonds to a large pan and toast for 5 minutes, before placing to one side
2. Add the quinoa and cinnamon to a medium saucepan and cook over a medium heat until warmed
3. Add the milk and stir everything well
4. Allow the pan to reach boiling point and then reduce to a simmer, covering over and leaving for 15 minutes
5. Before serving, add the rest of the ingredients and stir well

Cauliflower Fritters

Serves 2
Calories – 313, carbs – 40g, protein – 11g, fat – 12g

Ingredients

- 2.5 tbsp olive oil
- 2 tbsp garlic, minced
- 1 onion, chopped
- 1 can of chickpeas, drained and rinsed
- 2 tbsp hummus
- Half a cauliflower head, cubed
- Salt and pepper

Method

1. Preheat the oven to 220C / 428F
2. Add the chickpeas to a large mixing bowl and add 1tbsp olive oil, stirring well
3. Line a baking tray with parchment paper and add the chickpeas on top
4. Cook for 20 minutes in the oven
5. Place the chickpeas in a food processor and blitz until you get a crumble consistency
6. Add the rest of the olive oil to a frying pan, over a medium heat
7. Add the onion and garlic and cook for 3 minutes
8. Add the cauliflower, stir well and cook for another 3 minutes, before covering the pan over and cooking until the cauliflower is soft
9. Transfer the mixture to the food processor and combine to create another crumble consistency
10. Create patties from the mixture
11. Add a little oil to a large frying pan, over a medium heat
12. Cook the patties for 3 minutes on each side
13. Serve with the hummus on the side

Healthy Morning Pizza

Serves 2
Calories – 803, carbs – 41g, protein – 33g, fat – 60g

Ingredients

♦ 2 tbsp olive oil
♦ 4 slices bacon
♦ 4 eggs, beaten
♦ Half a chopped onion
♦ 2 tbsp green pesto
♦ 200g/7oz grated cheese
♦ 1 tomato, chopped

♦ 2 pitta breads, the round variety
♦ 3 mushrooms, chopped
♦ A few spinach leaves
♦ 1 avocado, pitted, peeled, and sliced

Method

1. Preheat the oven to 175C / 347F
2. Line a baking sheet with parchment paper
3. Cook the bacon in a large skillet pan over a medium heat
4. Transfer the bacon to paper towels, to blot the fat
5. Add the onion to the same skillet and cook for another 6 minutes, before placing to one side
6. Add the rest of the oil to the same skillet
7. Crack the eggs and stir, cooking for 4 minutes
8. Transfer the pitta bread to the baking sheet and add a little pesto to each side
9. Add the bacon on top, a little of the egg, tomato, spinach, and finally the mushroom
10. Add the cheese and season
11. Place in the oven and cook for 10 minutes
12. Serve with the avocado on the side

Courgette (Zucchini) With Eggs

Serves 2

Calories – 203, carbs – 11g, protein – 9g, fat – 13.5g

Ingredients

♦ 1.5 tbsp olive oil
♦ 2 courgettes/zucchinis, cubed

♦ 2 medium eggs
♦ Salt and pepper

Method

1. Cook the courgette/zucchini in the oil over medium heat until soft, seasoning to your liking
2. Beat the eggs in a medium bowl and pour over the courgette/zucchini
3. Cook until the eggs are to your liking
4. Season and serve

Breakfast Muffins

Serves 2
Calories – 135, carbs – 22g, protein – 14g, fat – 1g

Ingredients

- 2 egg whites
- 1 large tomato, sliced
- 2 wholewheat muffins, cut into two
- A few spinach leaves

Method

1. Use a medium pan to cook the egg whites for around 4 minutes
2. While you're waiting, toast the muffins a little and cut into halves
3. Add half the egg white to one muffin bottom section and add the rest to the other
4. Add a slice of tomato to each
5. Add a little bit of the spinach to each
6. Season and add the top of the muffin

Mediterranean Diet Lunch Recipes

Fuelling up at lunchtime is important. By eating a healthy meal, packed with nutritious vitamins and minerals, you'll have enough energy to get you through the afternoon, without resorting to sugary snacks and other unhealthy options.

As before, vary your meals and make sure that you try something new! If you've never had couscous before, give it a go. Never tried gazpacho? Trust us, it's delicious!

Here are some wonderful lunchtime meals that work well with the Mediterranean Diet.

Healthy Fishsticks

Serves 4
Calories – 180, carbs – 4g, protein – 3g, fat – 8g

Ingredients

- 2 tbsp olive oil
- 0.5kg/1.5lb skinless fish fillet (cod or salmon work well)
- 100g/0.5 cups all purpose flour
- 1 beaten egg
- 100g/0.5 cups of breadcrumbs
- 100g/0.5 cups of parmesan cheese
- Zest of 1 lemon and juice
- 1 tsp pepper
- 1 tsp sweet paprika
- 1 tsp dried oregano
- Salt and pepper for seasoning

Method

1. Preheat the oven to 220C/450F
2. Coat the fish with salt on both sides and cut into sticks, around 3" long
3. Take a bowl and add the oregano, paprika, and pepper, combining well
4. Cover both sides of the fish sticks with the mixture
5. Coat each fish stick first in the flour and shake off the excess
6. Dip into the egg wash and then the breadcrumbs
7. Finally, dip the fish sticks into the parmesan and pat both sides
8. Take a baking tray and cover with parchment paper
9. Arrange the sticks on the sheet and brush with the olive oil
10. Bake in the oven for 12-15 minutes
11. Serve with the lemon zest and juice over the top

Roasted Veggies, Italian Style

Serves 6
Calories – 200, carbs – 3g, protein – 6g, fat – 9g

Ingredients

- 2 tbsp olive oil
- 8 mushrooms, trimmed
- 12 baby potatoes, halved
- 12 cherry tomatoes
- 2 courgette/zucchini, cut into 1" pieces
- 12 garlic cloves
- 0.5 tsp dried oregano
- 1 tsp dried thyme
- Salt and pepper to season

Method

1. Preheat the oven to 220C / 425F
2. Take a large bowl and add the mushrooms, potatoes, tomatoes, courgette/zucchini, and garlic
3. Add the oil and toss to coat
4. Add the thyme, oregano, salt, and pepper and combine well
5. Place in the oven for 30 minutes
6. Serve while still warm

Greek Black Eyed Peas

Serves 6
Calories – 200, carbs – 2.5g, protein – 4g, fat – 8g

Ingredients

- 2 tbsp olive oil
- 1 onion, chopped
- 1 green bell pepper, chopped
- 4 garlic cloves, chopped
- 2 carrots, chopped
- 1 can of diced tomatoes
- 1 dry bay leaf
- 500ml/2 cups of water
- 2 cans of black eyed peas, drained
- The juice of 1 lemon
- 1.5 tsp ground cumin
- 1 tsp dry oregano
- 0.5 tsp paprika
- A handful of chopped, fresh parsley leaves
- Salt and pepper for seasoning

Method

1. Take a large saucepan and add the olive oil, cooking over a medium heat until warm
2. Add the garlic and onions and sauté for a few minutes
3. Add the carrots and peppers and cook for 5 minutes
4. Add the tomatoes, bay leaf, water, spices, and salt and pepper to season
5. Allow to boil for 5 minutes and then turn down the heat to simmer for 30 minutes, stirring occasionally
6. Add the lemon juice and the parsley and combine carefully before serving

Mediterranean Tuna Quiche

Serves 6
Calories – 200, carbs – 4.2g, protein – 7g, fat – 9g

Ingredients

- 1 courgette/zucchini, grated
- 1 onion, grated
- 1 carrot, grated
- 3 eggs
- 3 tbsp oats
- 1 can of tuna, drained
- 3 tbsp cream cheese
- 1 tbsp basil
- 1 tbsp dill
- Salt and pepper for seasoning

Method

1. Preheat the oven to 180C/350F
2. Take a bowl and mix together the cream cheese and eggs until smooth
3. Add the rest of the ingredients and combine well
4. Season a little and combine again
5. Take a baking pan and line with parchment paper
6. Transfer the mixture to the pan and cook in the oven for 20 minutes
7. Wait for the quiche to cool before removing from the pan and slicing

Pumpkin Frittata

Serves 4
Calories – 180, carbs – 3.9g, protein – 6g, fat – 8g

Ingredients

- 1 tbsp butter, plus an extra 1 tbsp for greasing
- 10 eggs, beaten
- 1 leek, sliced
- 1 onion, sliced
- 1 small bunch of asparagus, chopped
- 600g/3 cups pumpkin, chopped
- 1 tbsp chives, chopped
- Salt & pepper for seasoning

Method

1. Preheat the oven to 220C/450F
2. Take a frying pan and melt the butter over a low heat
3. Add the leeks, asparagus, and onion and cook for 5 minutes
4. Remove the pan and place to one side
5. Take a baking try and grease with butter
6. Transfer the mixture into the tray and add the pumpkin and chives, combining carefully
7. Pour the beaten eggs over the tray
8. Turn the oven down to 180C/380F and cook for 40 minutes

Pineapple & Teriyaki Chicken Salad

Serves 6

Calories – 200, carbs – 4.2g, protein – 7g, fat – 9g

Ingredients

- 2 chicken breasts
- 100g/0.5 cups of cooked quinoa
- 2 small avocados, flesh scooped out
- 1 tsp honey
- 1 tsp sesame seeds
- 3 tbsp tamari sauce
- 12 cherry tomatoes, halved
- Half a small pineapple, peeled and sliced into 1cm slices
- 1 baby lettuce, sliced

Method

1. Take a large bowl and combine the honey, 1 tsp sesame seeds, and the honey
2. Add the chicken to the bowl and combine
3. Let the chicken marinade for 5 minutes
4. Take a large frying pan and heat over a high temperature. Cook the pineapple for 1 minute, turn and cook on the other side
5. Place the pineapple to one side
6. Add the chicken to the pineapple plan and cook on a medium to high temperature for 6 minutes
7. Arrange the sliced lettuce on serving plates and top with a little quinoa on each
8. Add the avocado on top
9. Slice the chicken and place on top of the salad
10. Serve with sesame seeds

Chicken With Pecan & Pepper Sauce

Serves 4
Calories – 220, carbs – 4g, protein – 7g, fat – 7g

Ingredients

- 2 tbsp olive oil
- 0.5kg/1lb chicken cutlets
- 2 red bell peppers
- 1 tomato
- 1 tbsp red wine vinegar
- 1 clove of garlic
- 0.75 tsp salt
- 0.5 tsp ground pepper
- 0.25 tsp crushed red pepper
- A handful of chopped, toasted pecans

Method

1. Preheat your grill and cook the tomato and peppers until charred and blistered. Transfer to a plate
2. Take the chicken and season with salt and pepper
3. Place the chicken on the grill and cook for 8 minutes, turning occasionally
4. Once cooked, transfer on a plate and cover with foil to rest for 10 minutes
5. Take the peppers and tomatoes and remove the skins and seeds. Place in a blender with the garlic, oil, vinegar, pecans, crushed red pepper and a little salt and pepper. Pulse until smooth, for around 1 minute
6. Serve the chicken with the sauce on the side

Spicy Aubergine/Eggplant

Serves 6
Calories – 120, carbs – 2g, protein – 4g, fat – 6g

Ingredients

- 1 aubergine/eggplant, cut into cubes
- 2 tbsp olive oil
- 1 onion, chopped
- 1 green bell pepper, chopped
- 1 carrot, chopped
- 6 garlic cloves, minced
- 2 dry bay leaves
- 1 can of chopped tomatoes
- 2 cans of chickpeas, liquid reserved
- 1 tsp ground coriander
- 1 tsp dry oregano
- 0.75 tsp ground cinnamon
- 0.5 tsp ground turmeric
- Salt and pepper for seasoning

Method

1. Preheat the oven to 220C/400F
2. Take a large bowl and place the aubergine/eggplant inside
3. Sprinkle liberally with salt and carefully remove from the bowl. Place on paper towels to rest for 20 minutes
4. Rinse the aubergine/eggplant and pat dry
5. Take a large braiser and add 2 tbsp olive oil, heating over a medium to high heat
6. Add the peppers, carrot, and onions and cook for 3 minutes
7. Add the bay leaf, a little salt, and the spices, combining ell and cooking for another minute
8. Add the tomatoes, chickpeas, chickpeas liquid, and the aubergine/eggplant, combining well
9. Allow to boil for 10 minutes and then remove from the heat and place in the oven
10. Cook in the oven for 45 minutes
11. Serve with a drizzle of olive oil on top

Barley & Vegetables

Serves 6
Calories – 180, carbs – 3.2g, protein – 3g, fat – 9g

Ingredients

- 2 tbsp olive oil
- 165g/1 cup of pearl barley, washed and drained
- 1 red bell pepper, diced
- 1 yellow bell pepper, diced
- 1 red onion, diced
- 2 courgettes/zucchini, diced
- 2 spring onions/green onions, chopped
- 1 garlic clove, minced
- 2 tbsp fresh lemon juice
- A handful of fresh parsley, chopped
- 2 tsp harissa spice
- 0.75 tsp smoked paprika
- 500ml/2 cups of water

Method

1. Preheat the oven to 220C/425F
2. Take a large saucepan and add the water and pearl barley
3. Bring the pan to the boil and then turn down to simmer for 45 minutes
4. Meanwhile, take a large baking sheet and add the vegetables. Season with a little salt and pepper, half of the harissa spice and half of the smoked paprika. Drizzle with a little oil and combine everything well
5. Make sure all the vegetables are in one even layer and cook in the oven for 25 minutes
6. Once the pearl barley is cooked, drain and season with salt, pepper, and the rest of the harissa spice and smoked paprika, combining well
7. Place the pearl barley in a mixing bowl and add the vegetables, spring onions/scallions, parsley, and garlic. Combing well
8. Add the lemon juice and a little extra olive oil, combining again

Barley & Mushroom Soup

Serves 4
Calories – 220, carbs – 3g, protein – 5g, fat – 7g

Ingredients

- 2 tbsp olive oil
- 200g/1 cup of pearl barley
- 10 mushrooms, sliced
- 1 onion, chopped
- 2 celery stalks, chopped
- 4 garlic cloves, chopped
- 1 carrot, chopped
- 1 can of crushed tomatoes
- 1 tsp coriander
- 0.5 tsp cumin
- 0.5 tsp smoked paprika
- A handful of chopped parsley leaves
- 1000ml/6 cups of vegetable broth

Method

1. Take a large saucepan and add the olive oil over a medium heat
2. Add the mushrooms and cook for 5 minutes
3. Remove the mushrooms from the pan and place to one side
4. In the post, add a little more oil and cook the celery, garlic, onions, and carrots for 5 minutes, seasoning with a little salt and pepper
5. Add the spices and crushed tomatoes and combine, cooking for 3 minutes
6. Add the pearl barley and broth, bringing to the boil for 5 minutes and then turning down to a simmer for 30 minutes
7. Add the mushrooms back to the pot and cook for 5 minutes, stirring well
8. Serve with the fresh parsley

Minestrone Soup, Vegetarian-Style

Serves 6

Calories – 280, carbs – 5g, protein – 5g, fat – 6g

Ingredients

- 3 tbsp olive oil
- 2 carrots, chopped
- 1 onion, chopped
- 4 garlic cloves, minced
- 1 courgette/zucchini, diced
- 200g/1 cup of green beans
- 1 tsp paprika
- 0.5 tsp rosemary
- 1 can of crushed tomatoes
- 1 bay leaf
- 3 springs of fresh thyme
- 1 can of kidney beans
- 1000ml/6 cups of vegetable broth
- A handful of parsley, chopped
- 400g/2 cups of ditalini pasta
- Salt and pepper to season

Method

1. Take a large saucepan and add the olive oil, warming over a medium heat
2. Add the onions, celery, and carrots and turn up the heat to medium-high and cook for 5 minutes, stirring regularly
3. Add the green beans and courgette/zucchini and combine again
4. Add the paprika, rosemary, and a little salt and pepper, combine again
5. Add the broth, thyme, bay leaf, and crushed tomatoes. Stir well and cover the pot, allowing to simmer for 20 minutes
6. Add the kidney beans, stir, and cook for another 5 minutes
7. Add the pasta and basil and combine
8. Remove the bay leaf and season if necessary before serving

Spicy Falafel

Serves 6
Calories – 180, carbs – 3g, protein – 3g, fat – 7g

Ingredients

- Cooking oil for frying
- 400g/2 cups of chickpeas, soaked overnight and drained
- A handful of fresh parsley, chopped
- 2 tbsp toasted sesame seeds
- 1 onion, cut into quarters
- A handful of coriander/cilantro leaves, chopped
- A handful of fresh dill, chopped
- 8 peeled garlic cloves
- 1 tbsp black pepper
- 1 tbsp ground coriander
- 1 tbsp ground cumin
- 1 tsp cayenne pepper
- 1 tsp baking powder
- Salt for seasoning

Method

1. Take a food processer and add the chickpeas, onions, garlic, spices, and the herbs. Mix for 30 seconds at a time, scraping down the sides in-between, until a smooth mixture is created
2. Place the mixture into a bowl or box and cover. Place in the refrigerator for 1 hour
3. Before cooking, add the baking powder and sesame seeds and stir in well
4. Use your hands to create 0.5 thick patties from the mixture
5. Take a large saucepan and add oil, until it's about 3 inches high up the sides
6. Over a medium to high heat, wait until the oil is bubbling and then place the patties into the oil
7. Cook for 5 minutes, until brown and crispy
8. Remove from the pan and place on paper towels to drain the oil away
9. Serve while still warm

Spinach & Chicken Patties

Serves 4
Calories – 210, carbs – 3.5g, protein – 5g, fat – 9g

Ingredients

- 3 tbsp olive oil
- 0.5kg/1lb ground chicken
- 200g/1 cup of baby spinach, chopped
- 1 onion, diced
- 1 tbsp garlic, minced
- 100g/0.5 cups of breadcrumbs
- 3 tbsp Greek yogurt
- 1 tbsp fresh lemon juice
- A small handful of fresh dill, chopped
- 1 tsp dried oregano
- 0.5 tsp ground cumin
- 0.5 tsp paprika
- 0.5 tsp salt
- 0.25 tsp ground black pepper

Method

1. Take a large skillet pan and add 2 tbsp of olive oil, cooking over a medium heat for 2 minutes
2. Add the garlic and onions for 3 minutes
3. Add the spinach to the pan and cook for 1 minute
4. Empty the contents onto a plate and leave to on side to rest for 5 minutes
5. Take a mixing bowl and add the chicken, cooked spinach and onions, yogurt, breadcrumbs, oregano paprika, cumin, lemon juice, salt and pepper
6. Coming everything together
7. Use your hands to create patties out of the mixture – you should be able to make 12 patties
8. Add the rest of the olive oil to a skillet pan over a medium to high heat
9. Cook each patty for 5 minutes on each side
10. Serve while still hot and juicy

Coconut Curry Soup

Serves 6
Calories – 190 carbs – 4g, protein – 5g, fat – 7g

Ingredients

- 1 tbsp coconut oil
- 300g/1.5 cups of dry brown lentils
- 2 cloves of garlic, minced
- 1 onion, chopped
- 1 tbsp fresh ginger, grated
- 3 carrots, cubed
- 1 potato, cubed
- 500ml/2 cups of vegetable broth
- 300ml/1.5 cups of water
- 2 can of full fat coconut milk
- 1 tsp cumin
- 0.25 tsp turmeric
- 2 tsp garam masala
- 0.5 tsp curry powder
- 1 tbsp tomato paste
- Salt and pepper for seasoning

Method

1. Take a large bowl and add the lentils. Pour enough boiling water into the bowl to cover the lentils and allow to sit for 10 minutes
2. Take a large saucepan and add the oil, heating over a medium temperature
3. Add the garlic, onions, fresh ginger, and turmeric, combining well
4. Cook for 3 minutes and then add the curry powder, cumin, and garam masala. Combine and cook for another minute
5. Add the carrot, potato, lentils, tomato paste, vegetable broth, coconut milk, and water and combine
6. Bring the contents of the pan to the boil and then turn down to a low heat and allow to simmer for 15 minutes, with the pan covered
7. Once cooked, scoop one cup of the soup out of the pan and use a blender to combine
8. Return the blended cup to the pan and stir
9. Season and serve

Easy Mediterranean Salad

Serves 6
Calories – 200, carbs – 2.5g, protein – 4g, fat – 8g

Ingredients

- 2 tbsp olive oil
- 6 tomatoes, diced
- 2 tsp fresh lemon juice
- 1 cucumber, diced
- A handful of chopped parsley leaves
- 0.5 tsp black pepper
- 1 tsp sumac
- 1 tsp salt

Method

1. Take a large mixing bowl and add the cucumber, tomatoes, and parsley
2. Add the salt and combine
3. Allow the salad to rest for 10 minutes
4. Add the olive oil, lemon juice, and sumac and combine well

Vegetable & Egg Sheet Pan

Serves 6
Calories – 200, carbs – 4.2g, protein – 7g, fat – 9g

Ingredients

- 6 large eggs
- 1 tomato, diced
- 1 green bell pepper, sliced
- 1 red bell pepper, sliced
- 1 orange bell pepper, sliced
- 1 red onion, sliced
- 1 tsp cumin
- 1 tsp chili pepper
- 1 tbsp olive oil
- 1 handful of chopped, fresh parsley
- Salt and pepper to taste

Method

1. Preheat the oven to 204C / 400F
2. Take a large bowl and add the onion, peppers and combine
3. Add the spices and seasonings and combine again
4. Add the olive oil and toss to coat well
5. Take a large sheet pan and transfer the mixture in one even layer
6. Place in the oven for 15 minutes
7. Once cooked, carefully remove from the oven, and make six gaps in the vegetables. Crack an egg into each gap
8. Place back in the oven and cook for 5 minutes
9. Serve with diced tomatoes and chopped parsley

Egyptian Fava Beans (Foul Mudammas)

Serves 5
Calories – 220, carbs – 4g, protein – 9g, fat – 13g

Ingredients

- 1 tbsp olive oil
- 2 cans of fava beans
- 1 tomato, diced
- A handful of chopped parsley
- 2 chopped cloves of garlic
- The juice of one lemon
- 1 or 2 jalapeno peppers, chopped
- 1 tsp ground cumin
- 1 tsp salt
- 125ml / 0.5 cups of water

Method

1. Take a large skillet pan and add the water over a medium to high heat
2. Add the two cans of fava beans and mash down with a fork
3. Meanwhile, add the garlic and jalapenos to a dish and use a mortar and pestle to smash them down
4. Add the lemon juice and combine
5. Pour the mixture over the fava beans and add the olive oil, combining well
6. Add the tomatoes and parsley to serve

Cheesy Couscous With Vegetables

Serves 4
Calories – 421, carbs – 11g, protein – 10g, fat – 12g

Ingredients

- 1 tbsp olive oil
- 1 tbsp cornflour, with 1 tbsp water added to create a paste
- 250ml/1 cup vegetable stock
- 150g/5oz couscous
- 1 courgette/zucchini, sliced
- 1 green pepper, sliced
- 1 yellow pepper, sliced
- 1 red pepper, sliced
- 1 red onion, sliced
- 2 tbsp parsley leaves, chopped
- 250g/8.8oz halloumi cheese, sliced
- 2 tbsp red wine vinegar
- 0.5 tsp dried herbs
- 1 tsp garlic powder
- Salt and pepper

Method

1. Add the couscous to a large mixing bowl, add the vegetable stock, stir, and cover with plastic wrap
2. Add the red wine vinegar, herbs, a little salt, and the garlic powder to a large bowl, with 200ml/0.8 cups of water
3. Bring the pan to a simmer and then remove from the heat
4. Add the cornflour paste and stir well, adding back to the heat and cooking for another 2 minutes
5. Remove from the heat, add the parsley and combine once more
6. Add the remaining vegetables to a mixing bowl, season and combine well
7. Take a large griddle pan and add the olive oil over a high heat
8. Cook the vegetables for 5 minutes, turning and cooking for another 5 minutes
9. Cook the halloumi in the pan for around 6 minutes on each side, until charred
10. Stir the couscous with a fork and add the cooked vegetables and cheese, string well
11. Transfer to a plate and pour the red wine vinegar mixture over the top

Zingy Pasta Salad

Serves 1
Calories – 507, carbs – 71g, protein – 18g, fat – 18g

Ingredients

- 0.5 tbsp olive oil
- Juice and zest of one lemon
- 85g/3oz pasta (wholewheat), cooked to your preference
- 60g/2oz feta cheese, crumbled
- 1 red onion, chopped
- 100g/3.5oz cherry tomatoes, cut into quarters
- 1 cucumber, chopped
- 15g/0.5oz basil, chopped
- Salt and pepper

Method

1. Add the lemon zest and juice to a bowl with the oil, the red onion and a little seasoning, combining well
2. Add the pasta to the bowl and combine well
3. Add the basil, cucumber, and tomatoes, combining well
4. Add the feta and combine before serving

Mediterranean Panzanella

Serves 4
Calories – 208, carbs – 9.1g, protein – 9.3g, fat – 11.4g

Ingredients

- 4 tbsp olive oil
- 1 tbsp red wine vinegar
- 300g/10.5oz sourdough bread, cubed
- 500g/17oz tomatoes
- 1 tbsp capers, rinsed
- 55g/2oz olives, sliced
- Half a red onion, sliced
- A few fresh basil leaves
- Salt and pepper

Method

1. Combine the oil, capers, and basil in a food processor
2. Take a large mixing bowl and add half of the mixture to the bottom
3. Add the bread cubes and coat with the mixture
4. In a large bowl, add the majority of the tomatoes and allow the juice to squeeze out
5. Add the red onion, a little more oil and the olives and stir well
6. Transfer the caper mixture, vinegar and the bread into the main bowl and combine everything well
7. Serve with the rest of the tomatoes and season

Tuna Tortillas

Serves 2
Calories – 412, carbs – 34g, protein – 29g, fat – 11.5g

Ingredients

- 2 wholewheat tortillas
- 2 tbsp mayonnaise
- 2 medium eggs, boiled and cut into quarters
- 1 tomato, sliced
- 200g/7oz olives

- 4 gherkins, sliced
- 1 tbsp capers, drained
- 1 can of tuna
- 50g/1.7oz green beans
- 0.25 tsp dried, mixed herbs
- Salt and pepper

Method

1. Add the beans to a pan of boiling water and cook for 5 minutes, before draining and setting in a bowl of cold water
2. Add the herbs, capers, gherkins, and mayonnaise to a bowl and season, combining well
3. Add the drained can of tuna and stir well
4. Add a layer of spinach to each tortilla
5. Add the beans to each one and a little of the tuna mixture
6. Add a piece of egg to each one and a piece of tomato
7. Add the olives to each one
8. Roll the tortillas up and enjoy

Fruity Fennel Salad

Serves 4
Calories – 100, carbs – 9.3g, protein – 2.6g, fat – 13g

Ingredients

- 4 tbsp olive oil
- 1 orange, peeled and sliced (retaining the juice)
- 2 courgettes/zucchinis, sliced
- 2 tsp sherry vinegar
- 1 small lettuce
- 2 fennel bulbs, cut into small pieces
- Juice of half a lemon

Method

1. Take a large bowl and add the orange juice, vinegar, lemon juice, and olive oil, combining well
2. Take another bowl and add the slices of orange, fennel, courgette/zucchini, and lettuce, combining well
3. Add the juice mixture over the top and stir until well distributed
4. Serve

Vegetable Stuffed Peppers

Serves 2
Calories – 303, carbs – 11g, protein – 12g, fat – 14g

Ingredients

♦ 1 tbsp olive oil
♦ 100g/3.5oz goat's cheese, cut into cubes
♦ Zest of half an orange
♦ 1 red pepper, halved and deseeded
♦ 1 yellow pepper, halved and deseeded
♦ 1 onion, sliced
♦ 1 courgette/zucchini, diced
♦ 50g/1.7oz wholegrain rice, cooked and drained
♦ 75g/2.6oz halved cherry tomatoes
♦ 2 garlic cloves, crushed
♦ 1 tsp cumin
♦ 1 tsp ground coriander
♦ 3 tbsp chopped flat leaf parsley
♦ Salt and pepper

Method

1. Preheat your oven to 200C / 392F
2. Take a baking tray and line with parchment paper
3. Add the peppers onto the tray, leaving the open section facing up
4. Cook in the oven for 15 minutes
5. Heat the oil over a medium temperature in a large pan
6. Cook the courgettes/zucchinis and the onions for around 5 minutes, until soft
7. Add the tomatoes, coriander, garlic, and cumin and cook for a minute
8. Transfer into a large mixing bowl and add the orange zest, stirring well
9. Add the rice and parsley, season and combine again
10. Use a large spoon to add the mixture inside the peppers, to reach almost the top
11. Add a chunk of the cheese on top of each pepper
12. Cook in the oven for 10 minutes

Mediterranean Diet Acquacotta

Serves 4
Calories – 209, carbs – 13g, protein – 11g, fat – 14g

Ingredients

- 3 tbsp olive oil
- 850ml/3.5 cups chicken stock
- 5 medium eggs
- 3 slices of bread, shredded
- 50g/1.7g porcini mushrooms
- 1 can of plum tomatoes
- 2 red onions, chopped
- 2 garlic cloves, chopped
- 3 celery sticks, chopped
- 2 carrots, chopped
- 2 tsp thyme
- 2 tbsp chopped fresh parsley

Method

1. Add the oil to a medium frying pan and heat over a medium temperature
2. Add the garlic, celery, thyme, onions and carrots, cooking for 15 minutes
3. Take a large bowl and add the mushrooms, covering with hot water and setting aside for 20 minutes
4. Keep the liquid from the mushrooms once you remove them
5. Chop the mushrooms and transfer them into the pan, stirring well and cooking for 5 minutes
6. Add the tomatoes and cook for 15 minutes
7. Add the chicken stock to the pan and cook for 15 minutes more, turning down to a simmer
8. While the mixture is cooking, poach the eggs to your liking
9. Add the parsley and the bread to the main pan and stir well
10. When you serve the mixture, add a poached egg on top

Rich Tomato Soup

Serves 4

Calories – 202, carbs – 21g, protein – 9.4g, fat – 5.3g

Ingredients

- 1 can of chopped tomatoes
- 400g/14oz frozen vegetable mix
- 1 vegetable stock cube
- 50g/1.7oz ricotta
- 2 tbsp garlic, chopped
- 200ml/0.8 cups of water
- A few fresh basil leaves

Method

1. You will need a large soup pan
2. Add the garlic and half of the vegetable mix and stir well
3. Heat on a high temperature for around 5 minutes before adding the stock cube, basil, and tomatoes, combining well
4. Add the water and combine once more
5. Take a hand blender and create a smooth mixture
6. Add the remaining vegetable mix and cover the pan as it cooks for another 20 minutes
7. When serving, add a little ricotta over the top

Spanish Gazpacho

Serves 4
Calories – 206, carbs – 11g, protein – 2.5g, fat – 22g

Ingredients

- 75ml/0.3 cups olive oil
- 1 egg, boiled
- 2 slices wholewheat bread
- 50g/1.7oz ham, chopped
- 3 tbsp cider vinegar
- 8 large tomatoes, chopped
- 3 garlic cloves, chopped
- 1 green pepper, chopped and deseeded
- 1 red onion, chopped
- 100ml/0.4 cups of water

Method

1. Soak the bread in the water for half a minute on each side
2. Add the soaked bread, olive oil, garlic, tomatoes, and green pepper to a food processor and mix until you get a smooth consistency
3. Add the vinegar, 100ml of water and combine once more
4. Place the soup in the refrigerator for at least one hour before serving
5. When you do serve, add some of the ham and a little olive oil, along with a boiled egg

Hot & Herby Pasta

Serves 4
Calories – 606, carbs – 82g, protein – 21g, fat – 19g

Ingredients

- 2 tbsp olive oil
- 1 tsp cayenne pepper
- 75g/2.6oz blanched and chopped almonds
- 6 roasted garlic cloves
- 4 roasted red peppers
- 400g/14oz wholewheat pasta, cooked to your liking
- 50g/1.7oz parmesan cheese, chopped

Method

1. Add the cayenne pepper, almonds, garlic, parmesan, oil, and peppers to a food processor and combine until smooth
2. Combine the pasta with the pesto
3. Add the contents of the food processor to the pasta and combine well

Mediterranean Diet Dinner Recipes

By planning your meals every week, you'll be able to avoid that "no idea what to have for dinner" situation. All too often, these types of situations force people to call for a takeaway or grab the nearest unhealthy option and throw it in the microwave.

You can prepare a lot of these meals ahead of time and simply cook them when you return home from work/whatever else you need to do. Below you'll find a varied mix of different meals to create yourself. Go on, be brave and start cooking for yourself!

Vegetable Spaghetti Squash

Serves 4

Calories – 170, carbs – 3g, protein – 5g, fat – 9g

Ingredients

- 1.5 tbsp red wine vinegar
- 3 tbsp olive oil
- 75ml/1/4 cup of water, plus the same amount for the spaghetti squash
- A handful of fresh basil leaves
- A handful of fresh parsley leaves
- 1 clove of garlic
- 100g/0.5 cup of parmesan cheese, grated
- A handful of whole almonds
- 1 spaghetti squash
- 4 tomatoes, halved
- 200g/1 cup of cannellini beans
- Salt & pepper for seasoning

Method

1. Take a food processor and add the basil, parmesan, parsley, garlic, almonds, vinegar and a little salt and pepper. Combine until smoot, adding a little more oil if necessary
2. Add the water and combine again
3. Preheat the oven to 220C/400F
4. Take a baking sheet and line with foil
5. Cut the spaghetti squash in half and remove the seeds
6. Take a microwave-safe dish and add the spaghetti squash with the water and cook for 15 minutes until soft
7. Take a large bowl and add the tomatoes, oil, and some salt and pepper, combining well
8. Transfer the mixture to the baking try and place in the oven for 12 minutes
9. Add the beans to the tray and combine
10. Remove the flesh from the spaghetti squash and divide between your serving plates
11. Add some of the tomato mixture on top of each piece and a little of the pesto sauce

Vegetarian Sarma (Stuffed Cabbage Leaves)

Serves 4
Calories – 150, carbs – 3g, protein – 4g, fat – 5g

Ingredients

- 260ml/1 cup of water
- 100g/0.5 cups of brown rice
- 2 tbsp olive oil
- 1 large cabbage
- 4 garlic cloves, minced
- 0.5kg/1lb baby mushrooms, chopped finely
- 1 onion, chopped
- 1 can of crushed tomatoes
- 0.5 tsp dried rosemary
- 0.5 tsp dried rubbed sage
- A handful of dried currants
- A handful of toasted pine nuts, chopped
- 130ml/0.5 cups of red wine
- Salt & pepper for seasoning

Method

1. Take a medium sized pan and add the water, rice, and a teaspoon of oil
2. Bring the pan to the boil and reduce the heat down to low
3. Continue to cook until the rice has absorbed all the liquid
4. Transfer the rice to a bowl and place to one side
5. Take a baking sheet and line with kitchen towel
6. Fill a large bowl with boiling water
7. Remove the core from the cabbage and place the cabbage in the water and soak for 5 minutes
8. Remove the leaves as they become soft and place on the baking tray, patting with the towels to dry
9. Chop the remaining cabbage leaves finely
10. Take a large skillet and add half of the oil over a medium to high heat

11. Cook the onion, garlic, mushrooms, sage, rosemary and a little salt and pepper for 10 minutes, stirring occasionally
12. Add the wine and cook for 3 minutes, stirring occasionally
13. Transfer the mixture into the rice with the pine nuts and currants
14. Take a large skillet and add a little of the remaining oil
15. Add the chopped cabbage, a little salt and pepper, and stir until wilted
16. Add the rice mixture and combine
17. Take another skillet and the rest of the oil over a medium heat
18. Add the garlic, onion, and a little salt and pepper, cooking for 2 minutes
19. Add the wine and tomatoes, allowing the mixture to simmer until thickened, for around 10 minutes
20. Preheat the oven to 180C/375F
21. Take one large cabbage leaf and add a couple of spoons of the filling in the middle. Fold the sides over and roll up. Repeat with the rest of the large leaves
22. Place the rolled up leaves in a baking dish and ladle the tomato sauce over the top
23. Bake in the oven for 45 minutes

Chhole (Curried chickpeas)

Serves 4
Calories – 190, carbs – 3g, protein – 5g, fat – 9g

Ingredients

- 6 tbsp canola oil
- 1 serrano pepper, cut into three pieces
- 1 2" piece of ginger, chopped
- 4 cloves of garlic
- 1 onion, chopped
- 2 tsp ground coriander
- 2 tsp ground cumin
- 0.5 tsp ground turmeric
- 2 cans of chickpeas
- 1 can of canned, diced tomatoes
- 2 tsp garam masala
- Salt and pepper to taste

Method

1. Take a food processor and add the garlic, ginger, and serrano pepper and pulse until smooth
2. Add the onion and pulse until chopped
3. Take a large saucepan and add the oil over a medium to high heat
4. Add the onion mixture and cook for 5 minutes, stirring every so often
5. Add the cumin, turmeric, coriander and cook for 2 minutes
6. Add the tomatoes to your food processor and pulse
7. Add the tomatoes to the pan and season
8. Reduce the heat down to a simmer and cook for 4 minutes, stirring occasionally
9. Add the chickpeas and garam masala, combining well
10. Turn the heat down a little more and cover the pan for 5 minutes
11. Serve while still hot

Tarkari Soup

Serves 4
Calories – 170, carbs – 3g, protein – 7g, fat – 5g

Ingredients

- 2 tsp virgin oil
- 1 onion, diced
- 1 carrot, diced
- 2 cloves of garlic, minced
- 1000ml/4 cups of vegetable broth
- 1 can of chickpeas, rinsed
- 200g/1 cup of frozen peas
- 200g/1 cup of frozen corn
- A handful of spinach, chopped
- Salt and pepper to taste

Method

1. Take a large saucepan and add the oil over a medium heat
2. Add the garlic, onion, and carrot, cooking for 4 minutes and stirring occasionally
3. Add the chickpeas, broth, peas, corn, and a little salt and pepper
4. Bring the mixture to the boil and then reduce down to a simmer, cooking for 10 minutes
5. Add the spinach and stir until wilted, for about a minute
6. Serve immediately

Pistachio Nut Salmon

Serves 2
Calories – 220, carbs – 8g, protein – 3g, fat – 8g

Ingredients

- 2 salmon fillets
- 1 tbsp olive oil
- 1 garlic clove, minced
- 2 tbsp fresh lemon juice
- 0.25 tsp Dijon mustard
- 1 tbsp honey
- A handful of pistachio nuts, chopped

Method

1. Preheat the oven to 190C/375F
2. Wash the salmon carefully and pat dry
3. Take a baking tray and line with parchment paper
4. Place the salmon on the tray
5. Take a small mixing bowl and combine the mustard, lemon juice, honey, garlic, and olive oil
6. Use a brush to coat the salmon with the mixture
7. Add the chopped pistachios to the rest of the mixture in the bowl and combine
8. Use a spoon to heap the mixture on top of the salmon and press down slightly
9. Place in the oven for 20 minutes
10. Allow to rest for 5 minutes before serving

Beef Souvlaki Kebabs

Serves 2
Calories – 240, carbs – 4g, protein – 4g, fat – 4g

Ingredients

- 1kg/2lb sirloin steak, cut into 1.5" pieces
- 2 tbsp freshly squeezed lemon juice
- 3 tbsp olive oil
- 1 tbsp garlic, minced
- 1 red bell pepper, chopped
- 1 red onion, chopped
- 1 courgette/zucchini, chopped
- 2 tbsp Italian seasoning
- 1 tsp ground black pepper
- 2tsp salt
- 8 metal skewers

Method

1. Add the sirloin steak to a zip-lock bag, along with 2 tbsp olive oil, Italian seasoning, lemon juice, minced garlic, salt and pepper
2. Seal the bag and shake to coat the meat
3. Place the bag in the fridge for 30 minutes, or preferably overnight
4. Take the metal skewers and thread the beef onto the, mixing it up with peppers, courgette/zucchini, and red onion throughout
5. Brush the skewers with the rest of the olive oil
6. Preheat the grill to medium high heat and wait for 5 minutes
7. Grill the skewers for 8 minutes on each side, making sure the beef is cooked to your liking before serving

Italian Chickpea Soup

Serves 4
Calories – 180, carbs – 3g, protein – 8g, fat – 5g

Ingredients

- 2 tbsp olive oil
- 4 cloves of garlic, minced
- 1 onion, diced
- 2 tbsp tomato paste
- 1000ml/4.5 cups of vegetable broth
- 1 can of fire roasted tomatoes
- A handful of basil leaves, chopped
- 1 can of chickpeas drained
- 0.5 tsp dried oregano
- 0.5 tsp dried thyme
- 0.5 tsp red pepper flakes
- 1 tsp salt
- 150g/0.75 cups of rigatoni pasta

Method

1. Take a large saucepan and add the olive oil over a medium to high heat
2. Add the onion and cook for 6 minutes
3. Add the tomato paste and garlic and cook for another minute
4. Add the broth, tomatoes, basil, chickpeas, thyme, red pepper, flakes, oregano, and salt. Combine well
5. Bring the mixture to a simmer and turn down the temperature to medium -low for 10 minutes
6. Add the pasta and cook for 10 minutes
7. Season to your liking and serve. The longer you leave the soup to cool, the thicker it will become

Asparagus & Beef Risotto

Serves 4
Calories – 280, carbs – 5g, protein – 6g, fat – 7g

Ingredients

♦ 1000ml/4.5 cups of vegetable broth
♦ 1000ml/4.5 cups of water
♦ 3 tbsp olive oil
♦ 0.5kg/1lb asparagus, chopped
♦ 1 lemon – the zest from half, and the other half sliced
♦ 2 tbsp butter
♦ 1 onion, minced
♦ 400g/2 cups of arborio rice
♦ 0.25 tsp garlic powder
♦ 260ml/1 cup of white wine
♦ 200g/1 cup of grated Parmesan cheese
♦ Salt and pepper to season

Method

1. Preheat the oven to 204C / 400F
2. Take a large saucepan and combine the water, broth, and a little salt over al ow heat
3. Take a baking sheet and line with parchment paper
4. Place the asparagus onto the sheet and drizzle with a little oliv3 oil, season and add the zest from the lemon, mix together well
5. Place the lemon slices on top of the asparagus
6. Place the tray to one side
7. Take a medium pan and add the rest of the olive oil and butter over a medium heat
8. Add the onion and cook for 5 minutes
9. Add the garlic powder and rice, stirring regularly and cooking for 2 minutes
10. Add the wine and cook until all the liquid has disappeared
11. Place the asparagus in the oven and cook for 15 minutes
12. While the asparagus is cooking, add two large ladles of the broth into the risotto and cook until the liquid has disappeared, stirring occasionally
13. Every few minutes, add another ladle of the broth and keep stirring until the liquid has gone – stop when you have just two ladles left
14. Just before the rice has cooked, turn the heat down to low and add another two ladles of the broth and a little black pepper, stir well for 2 minutes until the risotto thickens
15. Add the asparagus and lemon wedges and serve while still hot

Chicken & Avocado Mashed Salad

Serves 2
Calories – 150, carbs – 3.5g, protein – 5g, fat – 7g

Ingredients

- 130g/2/3 cups of cooked chicken, shredded
- 1 avocado, chopped
- 1 garlic clove, minced
- 1 small red bell pepper, chopped
- 1 tbsp dill, chopped
- 1 carrot, chopped
- 1 red onion, chopped
- 2 cherry tomatoes, halved
- 5 olives, chopped
- The juice of half a lemon
- Salt and pepper for seasoning

Method

1. Place the avocado in a bowl and mash together with the garlic until smooth
2. Add the chicken to the bowl, along with the vegetables and the lemon juice
3. Season and combine well

Lemon & Garlic Cod

Serves 5
Calories – 190, carbs – 4g, protein – 6g, fat – 4g

Ingredients

- 5 tbsp olive oil
- 0.6kg/1.5lb cod fillet pieces
- A handful of fresh parsley leaves, chopped
- 5 tbsp fresh lemon juice
- 2 tbsp butter, melted
- 5 garlic cloves, minced
- 1 tsp ground coriander
- 0.75 tsp sweet paprika
- 0.75 tsp ground cumin
- 75g/1/3 cup of all purpose flour

Method

1. Preheat the oven to 220C/400F
2. Take a bowl and combine the olive oil, lemon juice, and melted butter. Place to one side
3. Take another bowl and add the flour, seasoning, and spices. Set aside.
4. Make sure the fish is dry and dip into the lemon sauce first, and then into the bowl containing the flour, shaking off any excess
5. Add 2 tbsp of olive oil to a skillet pan and warm over a medium to high heat
6. Add the fish and cook for 2 minutes on both sides
7. Remove the pan from the head and drizzle the lemon sauce over the fish. Add the mixed garlic and combine
8. Place the fish in the oven for around 10 minutes, until it flakes with a fork easily
9. Serve with chopped parsley over the top

Halibut & Veggies

Serves 6
Calories – 220, carbs – 4g, protein – 4g, fat – 5g

Ingredients

- 3 tbsp olive oil
- 0.7kg/1.5lb halibut fillet, cut into chunks
- 0.5kg/1lb fresh green beans
- 0.5kg/1lb cherry tomatoes
- 1 onion, cut into quarters
- Zest and juice of 2 lemons
- 1.5 tbsp minced garlic
- 2 tsp dill weed
- 0.5 tsp black pepper
- 1 tsp salt
- 1 tsp dried oregano
- 0.5 tsp ground coriander

Method

1. Preheat the oven to 230C/425F
2. Take a large bowl and combine the lemon zest and juice, olive oil, garlic, salt and pepper, oregano, coriander, and dill weed
3. Add the tomatoes, onions, and green beans and ensure everything is coated well
4. Take a large baking sheet and transfer the mixture in one even layer, covering just half of the sheet
5. Add the fish fillets to the bowl and coat with the rest of the sauce
6. Place the halibut on the baking tray, on the empty half, and drizzle any remaining sauce over the whole tray
7. Season to your liking
8. Bake in the oven for 15 minutes and then move to the top tray and cook for another 3 minutes, until the tomatoes pop open
9. Serve while still hot

Spicy Moroccan Fish

Serves 6
Calories – 250, carbs – 4g, protein – 4g, fat – 5g

Ingredients

♦ 3 tbsp olive oil
♦ 2 tbsp tomato paste
♦ 2 tomatoes, diced
♦ 8 cloves of garlic, 4 sliced and 4 minced
♦ 1 red pepper, sliced
♦ 350ml/1.5 cups of water
♦ 1 can of chickpeas, drained
♦ 0.7kg/1.5lb cod fillet pieces, around half an inch in thickness
♦ A handful of fresh coriander/cilantro
♦ 1.5 tsp Ras El Hanout
♦ 0.5 tsp cumin
♦ 0.75 tsp paprika
♦ The juice of half a lemon
♦ Half a lemon cut into thin slices
♦ Salt and pepper for seasoning

Method

1. Take a large pan with a lid and add 2 tbsp of the olive oil until warm
2. Add the garlic and cook until fragrant
3. Add the tomatoes, bell peppers and tomato paste, combining well and cooking for 3 minutes
4. Add the coriander/cilantro, sliced garlic, and chickpeas. Season a little and combine
5. Add 0.5 tsp Ras El Hanout spice and water and turn up the heat to a boil. Once boiling, lower to a simmer and cover for 20 minutes
6. Take a small bowl and add the rest of the Ras El Hanout spice, cumin, salt, and pepper, and paprika, combining well
7. Coat the fish with this mixture on both sides and a drizzle with a little olive oil
8. Add the fish to the pan, making sure it is covered with the sauce
9. Add the lemon juice and lemon slices and combine a little
10. Cook for 15 minutes

Shrimp With Mediterranean Peppers

Serves 4
Calories – 240, carbs – 4g, protein – 5g, fat – 10g

Ingredients

- 3 tbsp olive oil
- 0.5kg/1.25lb shrimps (you can use prawns if you prefer)
- 1 tbsp butter
- 1 tbsp all purpose flour
- 1 tsp smoked paprika
- 0.5 tsp ground coriander
- 0.5 tsp salt
- 0.5 tsp pepper
- 0.25 tsp cayenne pepper
- 0.25 tsp sugar
- 1 red onion, sliced
- 4 garlic cloves, chopped
- 1 green pepper, sliced
- 1 yellow pepper, sliced
- 1 can of diced tomatoes
- 2 tbsp dry white win
- 2 tbsp fresh lemon juice
- 100ml/1/3 cup of vegetable broth
- A handful of parsley leaves, chopped

Method

1. Wash the shrimp and pat dry
2. Take a bowl and add the flour, salt, pepper, coriander, smoked paprika, sugar, and cayenne pepper. Combine and coat the shrimp on all sides
3. Take a large skillet pan and melt the butter and olive oil over a low heat
4. Turn up to a medium heat and add the garlic and onions, cook for 2 minutes
5. Add the peppers and cook for another 4 minutes, stirring occasionally
6. Add the shrimp and cook for 2 minutes
7. Add the tomatoes, white wine, lemon juice, and broth. Cook for 2 more minutes
8. Add the parsley and serve

Tzatziki With Chicken Souvlaki

Serves 4
Calories – 190, carbs – 6g, protein – 8g, fat – 9g

Ingredients

- 3 tbsp olive oil
- 1kg/2.5lb chicken breast, cut into 1.5" pieces
- 10 garlic cloves, peeled
- 1 tsp salt
- 1 tsp black pepper
- The juice of 1 lemon
- 2 bay leaves
- 2 tbsp dried oregano
- 1 tsp sweet paprika
- 1 tsp dried rosemary
- 100ml/0.25 cups of white wine
- 5 tbsp tzatziki sauce
- 12 wooden skewers

Method

1. Take a large bowl and add the oregano, rosemary salt, pepper, paprika, garlic, olive oil, lemon juice and white wine. Take an immersion blender and pulse until the mixture is smooth
2. Take a large bowl and add the chicken inside and the bay leaves
3. Add the marinade to the bowl and make sur everything is coated. Cover and place in the refrigerator for 2 hours, or overnight if possible
4. Once the chicken is marinaded, thread onto the skewers
5. Brush the chicken with a little olive oil and cook on the grill over a medium to high heat until cooked, turning every 5 minutes
6. Allow the skewers to rest for five minutes before serving
7. Serve with tzatziki sauce ladled over the top

Garlic Swordfish

Serves 4
Calories – 250, carbs – 8g, protein – 9g, fat – 4g

Ingredients

- 3 tbsp olive oil
- 4 steaks of swordfish
- 12 garlic cloves, peeled
- 1 tsp coriander
- 0.75 tsp cumin
- 1 tsp sweet paprika
- 2 tbsp fresh lemon juice
- 0.5 tsp ground black pepper
- 1 tsp salt

Method

1. Take a food processor and add the lemon juice, olive oil, salt, pepper, spices, and garlic. Blend for 3 minutes until a smooth consistency is achieved
2. Take the swordfish steaks and pat them dry
3. Cover the swordfish in the marinade, coating on both sides
4. Set aside for 15 minutes
5. Heat a grill on a high heat and cook the swordfish on one side for 6 minutes and then turn over and cook for another 3 minutes
6. Serve with a little extra lemon juice

Tomato & Feta Shrimps

Serves 6
Calories – 190, carbs – 4g, protein – 5g, fat – 9g

Ingredients

- 0.6kg/1.5lb jumbo shrimp, deveined and peeled
- 2 tbsp olive oil, plus extra for drizzling
- 1.5 tsp dried oregano
- 1.5 tsp dried dill weed
- 0.5 tsp red pepper flakes
- 6 garlic cloves, minced
- 1 red onion, chopped
- 1 can of diced tomatoes
- Juice of 1 lemon
- A handful of mint leaves, chopped
- A handful of parsley leaves, chopped
- 50g/2oz feta cheese
- Salt and pepper for seasoning

Method

1. Dry the shrimp and place in a large mixing bowl
2. Season the shrimp with salt and pepper, 0.5 tsp dried oregano, red pepper flakes, 0.5 tsp dried dill weed and 0.5 tsp minced garlic, combing well
3. Drizzle a little olive oil and combine again. Place to one side
4. Take a large skillet pan and add 2 tbsp olive oil
5. Add the rest of the garlic and the onion, cooking for a few minutes, and stirring regularly
6. Add the lemon juice and tomatoes and combine again
7. Season with a little salt and pepper, as well as the rest of the dill and oregano
8. Allow the mixture to boil and then turn down to a medium to low heat and allow to simmer for 15 minutes
9. Add the shrimp to the pan and cook for 7 minutes
10. Add the parsley and mint leaves and combine
11. Add the feta cheese on top just before serving

Courgette (Zucchini) Sauteed Shrimps

Serves 4
Calories – 230, carbs – 5g, protein – 4g, fat – 10g

Ingredients

- 0.5kg/1lb large shrimps, deveined and peeled
- 2 tbsp olive oil
- 1.5 tsp dried oregano
- 1 tsp ground coriander
- 1 tsp ground cumin
- 0.5 tsp sweet paprika
- 5 garlic cloves, minced
- 1 courgette/zucchini, sliced
- 1 can of cooked chickpeas
- The juice of 1 lemon
- 10 cherry tomatoes, halved
- A handful of basil leaves, torn

Method

1. Take a small bowl and add the spices to combine
2. Dry the shrimp and season with salt and pepper
3. Add 1.5 tsp of the spice mixture and coat the shrimp, placing to one side
4. Take a large skillet pan and add 2 tbsp olive oil over a medium heat
5. Add half the garlic and the onions and cook for 4 minutes, stirring regularly
6. Add the courgette/zucchini, chickpeas, and peppers, combining well
7. Season and add the rest of the spice mixture, combining again
8. Cook for 7 minutes
9. Take a large plate and transfer the vegetables, pacing to one side
10. Place the pan back on the heat and add a little extra olive oil
11. Add the shrimp and the rest of the garlic, cooking over a medium to high heat, for around 5 minutes
12. Add the vegetables back into the pan and combine everything with the cherry tomatoes and lemon juice
13. Top with the fresh basil before serving

Fragrant Potatoes & Chicken

Serves 6
Calories – 230, carbs – 4g, protein – 8g, fat – 11g

Ingredients

- 1.3kg/3lb chicken legs/wings
- 4 potatoes, cut into wedges
- 1 onion, sliced
- 260ml/1 cup of chicken broth
- 5 tbsp olive oil
- 12 garlic cloves, minced
- 4 tbsp lemon juice
- 1 lemon, sliced
- 0.5 tsp ground nutmeg
- 1.5 tbsp dried rosemary
- Salt and pepper for seasoning

Method

1. Preheat the oven to 180C/350F
2. Dry the chicken and season with salt
3. Take a large baking dish and add the potatoes and onions in one even layer
4. Season with salt and pepper
5. Add the chicken to the dish and set aside
6. Take a small mixing bowl and add the lemon juice, garlic, rosemary, nutmeg, and olive oil. Whisk together until smooth
7. Pour the mixture over the potatoes and chicken
8. Place the lemon slices on top
9. Pour the chicken broth over the dish contents and place in the oven
10. Cook for between 45 minutes to 1 hour, until chicken is cooked

Chicken Shawarma

Serves 6
Calories – 190, carbs – 2g, protein – 5g, fat – 8g

Ingredients

- 8 chicken thighs, skinless and boneless
- 3 tbsp olive oil
- 1 onion, sliced
- Juice of 1 lemon
- 0.75 tbsp turmeric powder
- 0.75 tbsp ground cumin
- 0.75 tbsp garlic powder
- 0.75 tsp ground cloves
- 0.5 tsp cayenne pepper
- 6 pita pockets for serving
- Salt and pepper for seasoning

Method

1. Take a medium mixing bowl and combine the spices. Place to one side
2. Take the chicken thighs and pat to dry
3. Season with salt and pepper and slice into small pieces
4. Take a large mixing bowl and add the chicken
5. Transfer the spice mixture to the chicken bowl and combine well
6. Add the lemon juice, olive oil, and onions, and combine again
7. Cover the bowl and place in the refrigerator for at least three hours, or overnight if you have time
8. Preheat the oven to 220C/425F
9. Allow the chicken to reach room temperature before cooking
10. Take a baking sheet and grease with oil slightly
11. Add the chicken and onions to the tray in one even layer
12. Cook in the oven for 30 minutes
13. Serve in pita pockets while still warm

Mediterranean Red Lentil Soup

Serves 6
Calories – 150, carbs – 2g, protein – 3g, fat – 2g

Ingredients

- 3 tbsp olive oil
- 1 onion, chopped
- 2 carrots, chopped
- 3 garlic cloves, minced
- Half a can of crushed tomatoes
- 1.5 tsp cumin
- 1 tsp rosemary
- 0.5 tsp red pepper flakes
- 2 dry bay leaves
- 1600ml/7 cups vegetable broth
- 400g/2 cups of red lentils, washed and drained
- Zest and juice of 1 lemon
- Salt and pepper for seasoning

Method

1. Take a large saucepan and add the oil over a medium heat, until shimmering in the light
2. Add the garlic, carrots, and onions, combine, and cook for 3 minutes
3. Add the bay leaves and spices, combine, and cook for 10 seconds
4. Add the tomatoes, lentils, and the broth, combine well
5. Add the salt and pepper and combine again
6. Cover the pan and cook for 15-20 minutes, until the lentils are soft
7. Remove the pan from the heat and allow to cook for a few minutes
8. Use an immersion blender to create a smooth consistency
9. Add the lemon juice and zest, and stir through before serving

Salmon Soup

Serves 4
Calories – 180, carbs – 3g, protein – 4g, fat – 8g

Ingredients

- 2 tbsp olive oil
- 0.5kg/1lb salmon filled, cut into chunks
- 4 spring onions/green onions, chopped
- 4 garlic cloves, minced
- 1 green bell pepper, chopped
- A handful of fresh dill, chopped
- 0.5kg/1lb potatoes, sliced
- 1 carrot, sliced
- 0.75 tsp ground coriander
- 0.5 tsp ground cumin
- 1 tsp dry oregano
- 1200ml/7 cups of vegetable broth
- The zest and juice of 1 lemon
- Salt and pepper for seasoning

Method

1. Take a large saucepan and add the olive oil. Heat over a medium heat until shimmering
2. Add the pepper, onions and garlic and cook for 3 minutes
3. Add half of the dill and cook for 30 seconds
4. Add the potatoes, carrots, and broth and combine
5. Add the spices and season with salt and pepper, combining again
6. Bring the pan to a boil and then lower to a simmer for 5 minutes
7. Season the salmon with salt and add to the pot and cook until the salmon is cooked through
8. Add the lemon juice, zest, and the rest of the dill, and combine
9. Serve while still warm

Spicy Fish Casserole

Serves 2
Calories – 399, carbs – 21g, protein – 39g, fat – 4g

Ingredients

- 1 tbsp olive oil
- 500ml/2 cups of hot fish stock (cooked)
- 1 can of chopped tomatoes
- 2 pollock fillets, cut into large pieces
- 85g/3oz raw, shelled king prawns
- 2 celery sticks, diced
- 2 leeks, sliced
- 2 garlic cloves, chopped
- 2 carrots, diced
- 1 tsp fennel seeds

Method

1. You will need a large soup pan
2. Add the oil to the pan and warm over a medium heat
3. Add the fennel seeds, garlic, carrots, and celery, combining well and cooking until soft
4. Add the stock, leeks, and tomato, string well
5. Add the lid to the pan and bring to the boil
6. Reduce the temperature to simmer and leave to cook for 20 minutes
7. Add the fish ingredients and cook for 3 minutes, making sure everything is properly cooked

Balsamic Lamb With Vegetables

Serves 2
Calories – 403, carbs – 41g, protein – 31g, fat – 11g

Ingredients

- 2 tsp olive oil, plus 1 extra tsp
- 4 new potatoes, cut into halves
- 1 tsp balsamic vinegar
- 2 tsp rosemary, chopped
- 250g/8.8oz fillet of lamb
- 3 cloves of garlic
- 2 tsp capers, rinsed
- 1 red onion, sliced
- 6 olives, cut into halves
- 1 green pepper, sliced
- 1 aubergine/eggplant, sliced
- 1 carton of passata
- 1 bag of baby spinach

Method

1. Add the oil to a large frying pan, over a medium heat
2. Add the onion to the pan and cook for 5 minutes
3. Add the aubergine/eggplant to the pan and cook for 5 minutes more
4. Once the onion is soft, add the passata and combine well
5. Add the capers, the olives, balsamic vinegar and half of the rosemary, combining well
6. Cover the pan over and cook for 20 minutes, giving it a stir occasionally
7. Heat the oven to 170C / 338F
8. Boil the potatoes in a medium saucepan until soft, and then drain
9. In another bowl, add the garlic, the remaining rosemary and pepper, combining again
10. Rub this over the lamb evenly
11. Place the lamb inside a roasting time and cook for 20 minutes
12. Wilt the spinach in a pan and drain
13. Add the garlic mixture and spinach to the pan with the sauce inside and mix well
14. Serve the lamb with the mixture on the side

Seafood Paella

Serves 4
Calories – 506, carbs – 49g, protein – 29g, fat – 11g

Ingredients

- 4 tbsp olive oil
- 2 tbsp tomato puree
- 300g/10.5oz wholewheat rice, paella variety
- 250ml/1 cup of dry white wine
- 1.3 litres/5.5 cups of chicken stock
- 300g/10.5oz fresh mussels, cleaned
- 4 baby squid, sliced
- 12 prawns
- 1 clove of garlic, smashed
- 1 onion, chopped
- 2 celery sticks, chopped
- 1 tsp crushed fennel seeds
- 1 tsp smoked paprika
- A handful of chopped parsley

Method

1. Take a large frying pan and a quarter of the olive oil
2. Add the garlic to the pan and cook for a minute
3. Add the prawns and cook for 2 minutes
4. Add the squid, cooking for another minute
5. Add the mixture to a plate and place to one side
6. Add the rest of the oil to the pan and add the onion and celery, cooking for 15 minutes
7. Add the paprika, fennel seeds, and tomato puree, combining and cooking for 7 minutes
8. Take another pan and add the stock, bringing it to a simmer
9. Add the rice to the onion pan and stir well
10. Add the stock and wine to the pan and combine well
11. Bring to a simmer for 15 minutes and stir
12. Add the seafood to the pan as the rice is nearly cooked
13. Cover the pan and cook until everything is completely cooked through
14. Serve with parsley on the side

Seafood Traybake

Serves 2
Calories – 307, carbs – 21g, protein – 21g, fat – 15g

Ingredients

- 2 tbsp olive oil
- 1 sprig of rosemary, chopped
- 300g/10.5oz potatoes, sliced
- 2 fillets of sea bass
- 1 red pepper, sliced
- 25g/0.8oz olives, halved
- Half a lemon, sliced
- A few basil leaves

Method

1. Preheat the oven to 180C / 356F
2. Add a little oil to a baking tray and grease well
3. Add the potatoes and peppers on the tray in a single layer
4. Add a little oil over the top and combine well
5. Add the rosemary and combine well
6. Cook in the oven for half an hour, turning everything at the halfway point
7. Add the fish and the olives
8. Place a lemon slice on top of every piece of fish
9. Cook for10 minutes, making sure the fish is fully cooked
10. Serve with shredded basil leaves

Italian Meatballs & Spaghetti

Serves 4
Calories – 403, carbs – 61g, protein – 26g, fat – 10g

Ingredients

- 1 tsp olive oil, plus another 1 tbsp
- 250g/8.8oz minced pork
- 500g/17oz cherry tomatoes, halved
- 2 tsp tomato puree
- 250g/8.8oz spaghetti, wholewheat variety, cooked to your liking
- Half a tsp mustard, Dijon is best
- 1 garlic clove, crushed
- 2 garlic cloves, chopped
- 2 shallots, chopped
- 1 can of green lentils
- Half a tsp rosemary, chopped
- 1 tsp chilli flakes
- 125ml/0.5 cups of water

Method

1. Preheat the oven to 200C / 392F
2. Line a baking sheet with foil and brush a little oil over the top
3. Crush the lentils with a fork in a small mixing bowl
4. In a large bowl, add the pork, garlic cloves (all), lentils, pork, and the rosemary, stirring well
5. Create 20 meatballs from the mixture, making sure they're all even
6. Transfer the meatballs to the lined baking sheet and cook for 15 minutes
7. Add 2 tsp of oil to a large frying pan, over a medium heat
8. Cook the shallots for 4 minutes before adding the tomatoes and stirring
9. Add the tomato puree and water, bringing to a simmer and cooking for 2 minutes
10. Add the herbs and combine
11. Pour the mixture into a casserole dish and add the meatballs, covering with the sauce
12. Cover with foil and cook for 10 minutes in the oven
13. Serve with the spaghetti

Cheesy Chicken With Fresh Vegetables

Serves 4
Calories – 302, carbs – 31g, protein – 31g, fat – 7g

Ingredients

- 1 tbsp olive oil
- 4 chicken breasts
- 1 onion, sliced
- 20 cherry tomatoes
- 500g/17oz potatoes, sliced
- 85g/3oz cream cheese
- 4 garlic cloves, sliced
- 8 black olives, chopped
- A pinch of nutmeg

Method

1. Preheat your oven to 220C / 428F
2. Line a baking sheet with parchment paper
3. In a large bowl, cover the onion with boil water and allow to soak for 15 minutes
4. In another bowl, add the cheese, nutmeg, and spinach, stirring well
5. Take the chicken breasts and spread the cheese mixture over the top
6. Top with tomatoes
7. Drain the onions at this point
8. Take another mixing bowl and add the oil, garlic, olives, onions, and potatoes inside and combine well
9. Transfer the vegetables onto the baking sheet and cook in the oven for 25 minutes
10. Arrange the vegetable mixture into four even piles
11. Place a chicken piece over each pile
12. Cook in the oven for another 20 minutes, making sure the meat is fully cooked through

Mediterranean Chicken Paella

Serves 4
Calories – 600, carbs – 83g, protein – 38g, fat – 19g

Ingredients

- 3 tbsp olive oil
- 2 tbsp plain flour
- 400g/14oz paella rice (wholewheat)
- 200g/7oz peas (frozen works well)
- 1.5 litres/6.3 cups of chicken stock
- Zest and juice from 2 lemons

- 6 chicken thighs, seasoned
- 2 onions, chopped
- 3 garlic cloves, sliced
- 0.5 tsp saffron
- 1 tsp sweet paprika
- A few mint leaves, chopped
- A few dill leaves, chopped
- A few parsley leaves, chopped

Method

1. Preheat the oven to 180C / 356F
2. Cover both sides of the chicken thighs with the flour
3. Take a large frying pan with high sides and add 1tbsp of the oil
4. Brown the chicken in the pan and then transfer to a roasting tin
5. Place the tin in the oven to cook for 45 minutes
6. Using the same pan, add the rest of the oil and cook the onions and garlic for 10 minutes
7. Add the saffron, lemon zest, paprika, and the rice, stirring well
8. Add the stock and reduce the heat to a simmer, stirring occasionally. Cook for 20 minutes
9. Add the peas and lemon juice, combining well
10. Add the chicken thighs and remove from the heat
11. Leave the lid on the pan for 5 minutes before you serve

Vegetarian Lasagne

Serves 4
Calories – 309, carbs – 24g, protein – 18g, fat – 14g

Ingredients

- 3 tbsp olive oil
- 2 aubergines/eggplant, cut down the middle lengthwise
- 3 garlic cloves, chopped
- 2 onions, chopped
- 300g/10.5oz cooked butternut squash
- 1 can of tomatoes
- 125g/4.4oz mozzarella, torn into pieces
- 140g/5oz lentils, cooked
- A few basil leaves

Method

1. Preheat your oven to 220C / 428F
2. Brush each side of the aubergine/eggplant with half of the oil
3. Place the aubergine on a baking sheet and cook for 20 minutes, turning over at halfway
4. Add the rest of the oil to a large frying pan and add the onions, cooking until soft
5. Add the tomatoes and butternut squash, combining well
6. Cook for 15 minutes; you should see a thickened sauce appearing
7. Add the lentils and the basil and stir once more
8. In a small baking dish, spoon some of the mixture into the bottom to create an even layer
9. Add slices of aubergine/eggplant in another layer
10. Add another layer of the lentil mixture and another layer of the aubergine/eggplant
11. Top with the cheese
12. Place in the oven for 15-20 minutes

Spicy Steak Salad

Serves 2
Calories – 408, carbs – 40g, protein – 31g, fat – 14g

Ingredients

- 1 tbsp olive oil
- 300g/10.5oz steak, as lean as possible
- 85g/3oz pearl barley, rinsed and cooked
- Juice of half a lemon
- 1 red pepper, chopped
- 1 yellow pepper, chopped
- 1 red onion, cut into quarters
- Half a bag of watercress

Method

1. Once the pearl barley is cooked, drain and place into a large mixing bowl
2. Preheat the oven to 200C / 392F
3. Add the onion quarters to a large baking tray and add 1tbsp of olive oil on top, coating well
4. Place in the oven and cook for 20 minutes
5. Rub a little oil over both sides of the steak and season to your liking
6. Cook in a large frying pan for 5 minutes on each side
7. Remove and place to one side to rest
8. Transfer the peppers and onions to the barley and mix well
9. Add the watercress, lemon juice and seasoning, stirring again
10. Cut the steak into slices and serve on top of the salad

Stuffed Fish With Fennel

Serves 4
Calories – 429, carbs – 55g, protein – 31g, fat – 11g

Ingredients

- 3 tbsp olive oil
- 250ml/1 cup of chicken stock
- 200g/7oz couscous
- 2 sea bass fillets
- 1 onion, sliced
- 250g/8oz tomatoes, cut into halves
- 2 fennel bulbs, sliced
- 1 tbsp raisins
- Zest of one lemon
- 1 lemon, cut into wedges
- 2 tbsp pine nuts, toasted
- A handful of dill, chopped

Method

1. Preheat the oven to 200C / 392F
2. In a large roasting tin, add the fennel and onion with most of the oil
3. Combing everything well
4. Cook in the oven for 20 minutes
5. Add the couscous to a medium bowl
6. Add the stock and cover with plastic wrap for 15 minutes to soak
7. Take the fish and cut two slits into each side
8. Season and add a little lemon zest to each one
9. Once the couscous has soaked, use a fork to separate and fluff up
10. Add the lemon juice, half the pine nuts, zest, dill and a little seasoning to the couscous and combine
11. Stuff the fish with the mixture and transfer to the roasting tin
12. Add the raisins and tomatoes and combine well
13. Cook in the oven for half an hour, making sure everything is cooked through

Mediterranean Diet Dessert Recipes

If you thought being healthy meant no more desserts, think again! You can easily recreate some of your favourite mainstream desserts by adapting them to the Mediterranean way. If you love chocolate brownies, you'll be delighted to find a healthier recipe in this section!

While you don't necessarily have to have a dessert every single day, you can rest assured that these particular options will not ruin your efforts and will give you that sugar kick you may have been craving.

Decadent Chocolate Mousse

Serves 4

Calories – 308, carbs – 21g, protein – 13g, fat – 9g

Ingredients

- 100g/3.5oz good quality dark chocolate
- 500ml/2 cups of Greek yogurt
- 1 tbsp honey
- 180ml/0.7 cups of milk
- 0.5 tsp vanilla extract

Method

1. Add the milk and chocolate to a large pan and heat until the chocolate melts
2. Add the vanilla and honey, mixing everything together until smooth
3. Transfer the mixture to a large bowl with the yogurt and combine again
4. Distribute between the serving bowl and place in the refrigerator for 2 hours at least

Delicious Chocolate Brownies

Serves 8
Calories – 450, carbs – 33g, protein – 31g, fat – 33g

Ingredients

- 2 medium eggs
- 65g/2oz flour
- 0.5 tsp baking powder
- 50g/1.7oz cocoa powder
- 20g/0.7oz walnuts, chopped
- 95g/3.3oz sugar
- 60ml/0.2 cups of olive oil
- 32g/0.2 cups of Greek yogurt
- 1 tsp vanilla extract
- Pinch of salt

Method

1. Preheat the oven to 220C / 428F
2. Add the sugar and olive oil to a mixing bowl and combine well
3. Add the vanilla and combine
4. In another mixing bowl, add the eggs and beat until smooth
5. Add the sugar mixture and combine until totally smooth
6. Add the yogurt and combine again
7. Take another bowl and add the flour, baking powder, cocoa powder and combine well
8. Transfer the other mixture and combine once more
9. Add the nuts
10. Line a 9" baking tin with parchment paper
11. Transfer the mixture into the pan
12. Cook in the oven for 25 minutes
13. Cut into squares once cooled

Spicy Apple Cake

Serves 12
Calories – 330, carbs – 31g, protein – 12g, fat – 11g

Ingredients

- 230ml/0.9 cups of olive oil
- Juice of two oranges
- 2 eggs
- 128g/4.5oz sugar
- 1 tsp baking powder
- 1 tsp baking soda

- 380g/13oz wholewheat flour
- 2 large apples, chopped
- 95g/3.3oz raisins
- 0.5 tsp cinnamon
- 0.5 tsp nutmeg

Method

1. Preheat the oven to 220C / 428F
2. Add the apples to a large bowl and pour the orange juice over the top
3. Take another mixing bowl and add the cinnamon, flour, nutmeg, baking soda and baking powder
4. Mix together the olive oil and sugar until smooth
5. Slowly add the eggs and combine for another 2 minutes
6. Create a hole in the middle of the bowl containing the dry ingredients
7. Pour the egg mixture into the hole and stir carefully with a wooden spoon
8. Drain the apples and add to the mixture with the raisins, combining well
9. Line a 9" tin with parchment paper
10. Pour the mixture into the tin
11. Cook in the oven for 45 minutes

Mock Creme Brule

Serves 4
Calories – 310, carbs – 30g, protein – 31g, fat – 21g

Ingredients

- 260g/9oz ricotta cheese
- 2 tbsp sugar
- 2 tbsp honey
- 1 tbsp lemon zest

Method

1. Take a large bowl and add the ricotta, honey, lemon zest and combine well
2. You will need four ramekin dishes, on a flat baking tray
3. Divide the mixture equally between the dishes
4. Sprinkle a little sugar over the top
5. Place in the oven for between 5-10 minutes, until the tops are very hot and brown
6. Allow to cool for 10 minutes

Shortbread With a Crunch

Serves 8
Calories – 410, carbs – 11g, protein – 14g, fat – 31g

Ingredients

- 118ml/0.5 cups of olive oil
- 125g/4.4 oz flour
- 150g/5.2oz hazelnut meal
- 1 tsp salt
- 40g/1.4oz brown sugar
- 40g/1.4oz powdered sugar
- Juice and zest of 1 lemon
- 1 tsp vanilla

Method

1. Preheat the oven to 230C / 446F
2. Combine the flour, sugar, hazelnut meal, a quarter of the powdered sugar, salt, and lemon zest in a large bowl
3. Use a whisk to add the vanilla and olive oil o the mixture
4. Take an 8x8" baking dish and grease the inside
5. Pressure the dough inside the dish
6. Cook in the oven for 20 minutes
7. Cut the shortbread into squares
8. Allow to cool before taking out of the dish
9. Combine the lemon juice and the rest of the powdered sugar to create a drizzle
10. Pour over the shortbread while warm

Peanut Butter Bowls

Serves 4
Calories – 300, carbs – 42g, protein – 21g, fat – 9g

Ingredients

- 900ml/3.8oz Greek yogurt
- 32g/1oz peanut butter
- 2 bananas, sliced
- 1 tsp nutmeg
- 32g/1oz flax seed meal

Method

1. Take four even sized serving bowls and divide the yogurt between them
2. Add some of the sliced banana on top of each one
3. Melt the peanut butter in the microwave or on the hob
4. Add a tablespoon of the melted peanut butter over the top of each serving bowl
5. Sprinkle a little nutmeg and flax seed meal over each serving bowl

Healthy Choc Chip Cookies

Serves 12

Calories – 210, carbs – 11g, protein – 11g, fat – 20g

Ingredients

- 100g/3.5oz olive oil
- 100g/3.5oz brown sugar
- 80g/2.8oz tahini
- 150g/5.2oz chocolate, chopped into small pieces
- 200g/7oz wholewheat flour
- The juice of one orange
- 1 tbsp flax seeds
- 2 tsp vanilla extract
- 0.5 tsp baking soda
- 0.5 tsp cinnamon
- 0.5 tsp coffee powder (espresso)
- 0.5 tsp salt

Method

1. Add the flax seeds in a medium mixing bowl and add the orange juice. Place to one side
2. Add the tahini, oil, orange juice mixture, brown sugar, vanilla, coffee powder, cinnamon to a medium bowl and combine well
3. Add the salt and combine again, making sure that the sugar has dissolved
4. Add the baking soda and flour to another bowl
5. Fold the flour into the other bowl with a plastic spatula
6. Add the chocolate and combine once more
7. Place the bowl in the refrigerator for at least 4 hours
8. Preheat the oven to 185C / 365F
9. Line a baking sheet with parchment paper
10. Remove the dough from the refrigerator
11. Cook into 12 even pieces
12. Roll each piece into a ball and place on the tray
13. Cook in the oven for 12 minutes

Berry & Honey Yogurt

Serves 4
Calories – 200, carbs – 12g, protein – 10g, fat – 15g

Ingredients

- 128g/4.5oz raspberries
- 128g.4.5oz blueberries
- 157ml/0.6 cups of Greek yogurt
- 8 strawberries, cut into quarters
- 1 tbsp balsamic vinegar
- 2 tsp honey

Method

1. Coming the raspberries and blueberries with the balsamic vinegar in a large bowl
2. Set aside for 10 minutes
3. In another bowl, add the yogurt and honey and mix together well
4. Take four bowls and add the berries to each one, in equal measures
5. Add the yogurt on top of each serving bowl

Berry Ice Lollies

Serves 8
Calories – 154, carbs – 9g, protein – 2.6g, fat – 11.4g

Ingredients

♦ 150ml/0.6 cups of almond milk   ♦ 300g/10.5oz strawberries

Method

1. Wash the strawberries well and pat dry
2. Add the berries to the blender and pour in the almond milk
3. Blend until you get a smooth mixture
4. You will need popsicle moulds for the next step
5. Transfer the mixture into the moulds
6. Freeze for four hours at least

Maple Syrup Pears

Serves 4
Calories – 220, carbs – 11.5g, protein – 5.4g, fat – 21g

Ingredients

- 4 large pears
- 120ml/0.5 cups of maple syrup
- 0.25 tsp cinnamon
- 1 tsp vanilla extract

Method

1. Preheat the oven to 190C / 374F
2. Line a baking tray with parchment paper
3. Cut the pears into halves and cut a little of the underneath so they're able to stand on the tray more easily
4. Scoop out the flesh of the pears with a spoon and remove the seeds too
5. Place the pears on the baking sheet, with the scooped out middle facing up
6. Add a little cinnamon on top of each pear
7. Combine the maple syrup and vanilla in a small bowl
8. Pour the mixture over the pears, keeping a little to one side
9. Cook the pears in the oven for 30 minutes, until soft and a little brown
10. Drizzle the syrup over the hot pears and serve

14-Day Mediterranean Diet Meal Plan

Now you've seen how delicious the Mediterranean Diet can be, it's time to look towards the practical side of things.

The recipes we've given you so far are easy to make, full of ingredients which you'll have no problems finding in the supermarket, and they won't break the bank either. Not only that, but these recipes are packed with vitamins and minerals, including all the nutrition you need for a healthy mind, body, and soul.

However, whenever you start a new eating regime, it's a good idea to have a plan to get you started. It's easy to become confused or accidentally start eating too much of the wrong thing from the start. That's why we've put together a handy 14-day plan to get you off to the best possible start in your Mediterranean Diet journey.

Below you'll find 14 days' worth of meals, including a breakfast, lunch, and dinner. You'll notice that we included a dessert section in the book, and if you feel like enjoying a dessert on any given day, you can incorporate that too, provided you stick to either the recipes we've given you, or you make sure that whatever you have is made of fresh, Mediterranean Diet-approved ingredients and that it's not packed with a huge amount of fat or sugar.

Remember to drink plenty of water every single day and if you want to, you can have one small glass of wine. If you don't like one particular meal, we've shown you for a particular day, that's fine. You can mix and match however you like, but make sure that you stay within the guidelines we talked about in our introductory section, to avoid accidentally moving into the 'unhealthy 'realm'.

The great thing about the Mediterranean diet is that it's not only packed with delicious meals, but that it's also very flexible. Once you've got the basics down-pat, you'll find it easy to mix and match and find meals which fit the guidelines and offer you delicious alternatives to the types of foods that perhaps you don't like so much.

You can also add one of the dessert recipes onto any day you like. Remember, the recipes in this book are all designed to fit in with the Mediterranean Diet, so there are no issues with going over your allowance. This particular diet doesn't ask you to weigh or limit anything; it simply asks you to eat in a healthier way than you have before, by making sensible choices. So, if you're craving something sweet, add a dessert to your daily meal plan.

Now, if you're ready, let's get started with day 1 of your Mediterranean journey!

DAY 1

Breakfast – Spinach & artichoke pancake (See page 23)

Lunch – Falafel Flatbread

Serves 9

Calories – 114, carbs – 11g, protein – 3g, fat – 2g

Ingredients

- 1 tbsp olive oil
- 70g/2.4oz chickpea flour
- 128g/4.5oz chickpeas, soaked and drained
- 70g/2.4oz onion, chopped
- 3 tbsp water
- 70g/2.4oz chopped coriander/ cilantro
- 128g/4.5oz chopped parsley
- 3 garlic cloves
- 1 green pepper, chopped
- 0.5 tsp baking soda
- 1 tsp cumin
- 1 tsp salt
- 0.25 tsp pepper
- 0.5 tsp cardamom

Method

1. Preheat the oven to 220C / 428F
2. Take the chickpeas and drain away the liquid
3. Place the chickpeas into a food processor and blitz until grain-like
4. Add the salt, pepper, cumin, green pepper, garlic, onion, cardamom, coriander/cilantro, parsley, and baking soda to the food processor. Combine once more
5. Transfer to a large bowl and put into the refrigerator for at least one hour
6. Add the flour, water, chickpea flour and oil to the bowl and combine using your hands
7. Line a baking sheet with parchment paper
8. Transfer the mixture to the sheet and use your hands to press down firmly
9. Cook in the oven for 30 minutes
10. Slice the bread up once cooled

Dinner – Seafood paella (See page 96)

DAY 2
Breakfast – Potato Toast
Serves 2

Calories – 20, carbs – 3g, protein – 2g, fat – 0.5g

Ingredients

♦ A small amount of olive oil

♦ 1 large sweet potato, cut into slices

Method

1. Preheat the oven to 220C / 428F
2. Line a baking sheet with parchment
3. Arrange the slices of potato on the sheet
4. Drizzle a little oil over the potato
5. Cook in the oven for 30 minutes
6. Serve while warm

Lunch – Zingy pasta salad (See page 54)

Dinner – Balsamic lamb with vegetables (See page 94)

DAY 3

Breakfast – Shakshuka (See page 25)

Lunch – Tuna tortillas (See page 56)

Dinner – Healthy Chicken with Balsamic Vegetables

Serves 4

Calories – 421, carbs – 13.5g, protein – 21g, fat – 30g

Ingredients

♦ 4 tbsp olive oil
♦ 4 chicken thighs
♦ 12 Brussels sprouts
♦ 1 tbsp maple syrup
♦ 100ml/0.4 cups of balsamic vinegar
♦ 2 garlic cloves, minced
♦ 1 red onion
♦ Salt and pepper

Method

1. Whisk together the maple syrup, balsamic vinegar, olive oil (2 tbsp) garlic, and seasoning
2. Transfer the chicken thighs to a large mixing bowl and add the mixture on top, using your hands to make sure everything is evenly coated
3. Cover the bowl over with plastic wrap and allow to rest in the refrigerator for 2 hours
4. Preheat the oven to 220C / 428F
5. Take the red onion and cut into quarters
6. Cut the Brussels sprouts into halves
7. Add the sprouts and onions onto a baking sheet and drizzle a little olive oil over the top with some seasoning
8. Coat everything well
9. Add the chicken to the baking sheet and make sure the vegetables are around and not on top
10. Cook in the oven for 30 minutes, ensuring the meat is cooked properly
11. Take the mixture from the bowl the chicken was resting in and transfer to a pan, heating over a medium heat, swimming for 10 minutes
12. Brush the chicken with the mixture while it is still cooking

DAY 4

Breakfast – Fruity potato hash (See page 21)

Lunch – Creamy squash soup

Serves 4

Calories – 220, carbs – 51g, protein – 3g, fat – 2g

Ingredients

- 1 tbsp avocado oil
- 900ml/3.8 cups of vegetable broth
- 0.5 tbsp maple syrup
- 1 butternut squash, sliced lengthways
- 1 clove of garlic
- 1 onion, halved
- 0.25 tsp ginger
- 0.25 tsp nutmeg
- Salt and pepper

Method

1. Preheat the oven to 250C / 482F
2. Take the butternut squash and use a spoon to remove the seeds
3. Add the squash onto a baking tray, with the scooped out side facing up
4. Season and cook for 1 hour
5. After half an hour of cooking, add the onions on the tray and brush a little oil over the top, cooking for the rest of the hour
6. Once cooked, scoop the flesh of the butternut squash out of the middle and add into a blender
7. Add some of the onion to the blender too
8. Add the garlic, broth, ginger, maple syrup, and nutmeg to the blender and create a smooth consistency
9. Season and serve

Dinner – Spicy steak salad (See page 104)

DAY 5

Breakfast – Creamy Breakfast Oatmeal
Serves 1
Calories – 230, carbs – 31g, protein – 11g, fat – 0.5g

Ingredients

♦ 70g/2.5oz rolled oats

♦ 230m/0.9 cups of water

Method

1. Add the water to a large saucepan and bring to the boil
2. Once the water is boiling, add the oats and stir until everything is well combined
3. Reduce the heat and simmer for 5 minutes
4. If you want your oatmeal a little thicker, allow to cook for a few minutes more

Lunch – Vegetable stuffed peppers (See page 58)

Dinner – Spicy fish casserole (See page 93)

DAY 6

Breakfast – Morning vegetables & eggs (See page 20)
Lunch – Cheesy couscous with vegetables (See page 52)
Dinner – Ginger & Citrus Scallops

Serves 4

Calories – 204, carbs – 11g, protein – 19g, fat – 11g

Ingredients

- 2 tbsp avocado oil
- 700g/24oz scallops
- The zest and juice of 1 orange
- The juice of 1 lemon
- 2 tbsp butter
- 1 tbsp grated ginger
- Salt and pepper

Method

1. Season the scallops with a little salt
2. Take a large frying pan and add the oil, heating over a medium temperature
3. Add the scallops to the pan and cook for 2 minutes, before turning and cooking for another 2 minutes on the other side
4. Remove the scallops and leave to rest on a plate
5. Reduce the heat and add the orange zest, butter, ginger, and lemon juice
6. Stir everything and simmer for a few minutes
7. Add the scallops and ladle the sauce over the top
8. Serve with the extra sauce poured over the top of the scallops

DAY 7

Breakfast – Cheese & spinach breakfast casserole (See page 24)

Lunch – Tasty Salmon Patties

Serves 2

Calories – 410, carbs – 5.6g, protein – 21g, fat – 39g

Ingredients

- 4 tbsp olive oil
- 450g/15.8g salmon
- 70g/2.4oz almond flour
- 1 onion, diced
- 1 red pepper, diced
- 2 eggs, beaten
- 2 garlic cloves, minced
- 1 tbsp mustard, Dijon works well
- 2 tbsp mayonnaise
- 25g parsley, chopped
- 2 tbsp dill, chopped
- Salt and pepper

Method

1. Preheat the oven to 240C / 464F
2. Take a baking tray and arrange the salmon on top, drizzling with a little oil and seasoning to your liking
3. Cook for 13 minutes, making sure it's cooked completely
4. Once cooked, place in the refrigerator for around 10 minutes
5. Take a large frying pan and add a little oil, heating over a medium temperature
6. Cook the onion and peppers for 10 minutes
7. Transfer the onion and peppers to a plate
8. Remove the skin from the salmon and add to a mixing bowl, using a fork to flake the fish
9. Add the dill, onion, mayonnaise, pepper, eggs, garlic, mustard, parley and almond flour to the bowl and combine everything well – using your hands will yield better results
10. Create four patties from the mixture, using your hands
11. Take a large frying pan and add the rest of the oil
12. Cook for 4 minutes, turning and cooking for another 4 minutes on the other side
13. Remove from the pan and allow to sit on paper towels for 2 minutes before serving

Dinner – Italian meatballs & spaghetti (See page 99)

DAY 8

Breakfast – Salmon & Avocado Surprise
Serves 4 (3 per serving)
Calories – 41, carbs – 1.5g, protein – 4.5g, fat – 2.5g

Ingredients

- 170g/6oz smoked salmon
- 1 avocado, peeled and pitted
- 1 cucumber
- 0.5 tbsp fresh lime juice
- Black pepper

Method

1. Cut the cucumber into quarter inch thick slices and arrange on the serving plate
2. Add the avocado and line juice into a bowl and mash with a fork until everything is smooth and lump-free
3. Transfer a small amount of the mash on top of each slice of cucumber
4. Add a piece of salmon on top of each pile
5. Season with black pepper
6. Repeat until all the ingredients have been used

Lunch – Mediterranean panzanella (See page 55)

Dinner – Seafood traybake (See page 98)

DAY 9

Breakfast – Healthy morning pizza (See page 28)

Lunch – Fruity fennel salad (See page 57)

Dinner – Mediterranean vegetable skewers

Serves 6

Calories – 153, carbs – 10g, protein – 19g, fat – 2g

Ingredients

- 4 tbsp olive oil
- 3 tbsp fresh lemon juice
- 680g/23oz chicken breasts
- 1 tsp mustard (Dijon works best)
- 1 yellow red bell pepper, sliced
- 1 red bell pepper, sliced
- 1 courgette/zucchini, sliced
- 1 red onion, sliced
- 2 tbsp red wine vinegar
- 3 garlic cloves, minced
- 1 tsp oregano
- Salt and pepper

Method

1. Combine the red wine vinegar, mustard olive oil, garlic, lemon juice, oregano and seasoning in a large mixing bowl
2. Cut the chicken breasts into pieces and add into a bowl
3. Add the marinade to the chicken and combine well
4. Cover the chicken with plastic wrap and place in the refrigerator for one hour
5. Turn your grill up to medium
6. Using metal skewers, add the chicken, pepper, courgette/zucchini, and onion onto the skewers alternatively
7. Cook the skewers on the grill for 8 minutes
8. Turn and cook on the other side for another 8 minutes
9. Make sure the chicken is cooked through before serving

DAY 10

Breakfast – Cauliflower fritters (See page 27)

Lunch – Beets & ginger soup

Serves 4

Calories – 115, carbs – 19g, protein – 1g, fat – 2g

Ingredients

- 940g/33oz vegetable broth
- 3 beetroots, peeled and diced
- 2 tbsp olive oil
- 1 tbsp fresh ginger, chopped
- 3 garlic cloves, minced
- 1 onion, chopped
- 1 parsnip, peeled and diced
- Salt and pepper

Method

1. For this recipe you will need a large soup pot
2. Add the olive oil to the pan over a medium heat
3. Cook the onion for around 5 minutes, until translucent and soft
4. Add the garlic, ginger, seasoning. Cook for another 2 minutes
5. Add the beetroot and parsnips and combine well
6. Add the broth and stir everything together
7. Bring the mixture to a boil and then turn down to a simmer for 30 minutes, with the lid on the pot
8. Transfer the soup into a blender and combine until you reach the consistency you like
9. Season before serving

Dinner – Mediterranean chicken paella (See page 102)

DAY 11

Breakfast – Easy DIY yogurt
Serves 7
Calories – 95, carbs – 5g, protein – 4g, fat – 2.5g

Ingredients

- 1200g/2.5lb organic milk
- 1 packet of regular yogurt starter
- Thermometer for measuring the milk heat
- Yogurt making machine

Method

1. Add the milk to a large microwave-safe bowl
2. Place the bowl into the microwave and use a high setting. You need the milk to be at 82C / 179F
3. Remove from the microwave and allow to cool until it hits 46C / 114F
4. Remove 230ml/1 cup of the milk from the main bowl and transfer to a small glass
5. Add the yogurt starter to the glass and stir until totally combined
6. Transfer back into the main bowl and mix together well
7. Fill the yogurt maker glasses will the mixture and place inside, setting the timer for 9 hours
8. Remove and place the glasses inside the refrigerator

Lunch – Rich tomato soup (See page 61)

Dinner – Stuffed fish with fennel (See page 105)

DAY 12

Breakfast – Quinoa for the mornings (See page 26)

Lunch – Spanish gazpacho (See page 62)

Dinner – Pork & Fennel Meatballs

Serves 8

Calories – 91, carbs – 8g, protein – 2g, fat – 1g

Ingredients

♦ 5.5 tbsp olive oil
♦ 900g/1.9oz ground pork
♦ Half an onion, chopped
♦ 1 fennel bulb, chopped
♦ 4 garlic cloves, chopped
♦ 120g/0.3oz baby spinach
♦ 15g/0.03oz parsley, chopped
♦ 2 eggs, beaten
♦ 1 tsp fennel seeds
♦ Salt and pepper

Method

1. Add a quarter of the oil to a large frying pan, over a medium heat
2. Add the onion and half the fennel, cooking for 5 minutes
3. Transfer to a plate and set aside
4. Combine the pork, eggs, fennel seeds, parsley, and seasoning in a large bowl
5. Add the fennel and cooked onion and combine again
6. Use your hands to create around 35 meatballs from the mixture
7. Line a baking tray with baking parchment and arrange the meatballs on the tray to rest
8. Add almost all of the remaining oil to a large pan and arrange the meatballs in the pan
9. Cook for 3 minutes and then turn and cook for another 3 minutes on the other side
10. Remove to a paper towel to absorb the excess oil
11. Take another pan and add the last bit of the oil over a medium heat
12. Add the remaining fennel and cook for 6 minutes
13. Add the garlic and cook for another 4 minutes
14. Add the spinach, stir well
15. Serve the meatballs on a plate with the mixture to the side

DAY 13

Breakfast – Breakfast muffins (See page 30)

Lunch – Garlic & onion cabbage

Serves 6

Calories – 70, carbs – 4g, protein – 1.5g, fat – 4.5g

Ingredients

- 1 cabbage head, sliced thinly
- 2 tbsp ghee
- 2 garlic cloves, minced
- 1 onion, sliced
- Salt and pepper

Method

1. Add the ghee to a large skill and heat over a medium temperature
2. Add the onion and cook until soft
3. Add the garlic and cook for another minute, stirring well
4. Add the cabbage and cook for 20 minutes, giving it a stir every so often
5. Season and serve

Dinner – Cheesy chicken with fresh vegetables (See page 101)

DAY 14

Breakfast – Smoked salmon breakfast frittata
Serves 6
Calories – 306, carbs – 6.7g, protein – 21g, fat – 20g

Ingredients

- 3 tbsp olive oil
- 9 eggs
- 246g/8.6oz yogurt
- 113g/3.9oz goat's cheese
- 226g/8oz smoked salmon, cut into small pieces
- 1 leek, diced
- 3 spring onions/scallions, sliced
- 1 shallot, sliced
- 1 bunch of dill, chopped
- 1 bunch of parsley, chopped
- 1 bunch of chopped dill
- Salt and pepper

Method

1. Add 1 tbsp of the oil to a large pan and heat over a medium temperature
2. Add the spring onions/scallions, shallot, leek to the pan and cook for 4 minutes
3. Transfer the contents of the pan to a plate and allow to rest
4. Add the eggs and eggs to a large bowl and whisk together,
5. Add the goat's cheese, herbs, shallots, leek, and spring onions/scallions, with the salmon and mix together well
6. Add 2 tbsp of oil to the skillet and add the mixture into the pan
7. Cook for 10-12 minutes. The edges will start to set
8. Remove and place under the grill for another 10 minutes
9. Once cooled, cut into slices

Lunch – Hot & herby pasta (See page 63)

Dinner – Vegetarian lasagne (See page 103)

Conclusion

Now you're at the end of the book, how do you feel about the Mediterranean Diet? Hopefully you're ready and raring to go, eager to start recreating these delicious and healthy meals from scratch.

You can also see just how easy it is to make meals yourself, rather than always calling for a takeout or resorting to a microwave meal. You'll notice just how much healthier you feel after a few weeks, in fact after the first week you might even notice that you have more energy and feel a lot more alert.

Focusing on health and wellbeing is never a waste of time. Forget those fad diets you probably tried before. The fact you're reading this book tells us very clearly that they don't work for you. You're trying to find a healthy eating regimen that doesn't cause you to feel hungry, stressed, and downright miserable. Now you've found it!

The benefits of the Mediterranean Diet are plentiful. Just because the produce you need for these recipes is more freely available in Mediterranean regions doesn't mean you'll lack flavour or vitamins by choosing those you find in your local market or supermarket. Shop organic and choose your produce carefully. When you do that, you'll notice just how delicious your meals are and how much better you feel as a result.

Remember to throw in some exercise to make the most of that extra energy, drink plenty of water, and mix up your meals as much as possible. Variation is key in enjoying your food and you can see just how delicious this type of eating can be!

So, it's time to wave goodbye to old, unhealthy habits. Make today the day you change your life completely for the better. You don't have to live in the Mediterranean to enjoy the benefits of the food that grows there naturally. You just need to know how to make use of it!

EXCLUSIVE BONUS

40 Weight Loss Recipes

&

14 Days Meal Plan

Scan the QR-Code and receive
the FREE download:

Disclaimer

This book contains opinions and ideas of the author and is meant to teach the reader informative and helpful knowledge while due care should be taken by the user in the application of the information provided. The instructions and strategies are possibly not right for every reader and there is no guarantee that they work for everyone. Using this book and implementing the information/recipes therein contained is explicitly your own responsibility and risk. This work with all its contents, does not guarantee correctness, completion, quality or correctness of the provided information. Misinformation or misprints cannot be completely eliminated.

Printed in Great Britain
by Amazon

25414872R00081